PRINCES OF JADE

Edmund Capon & William MacQuitty

NELSON

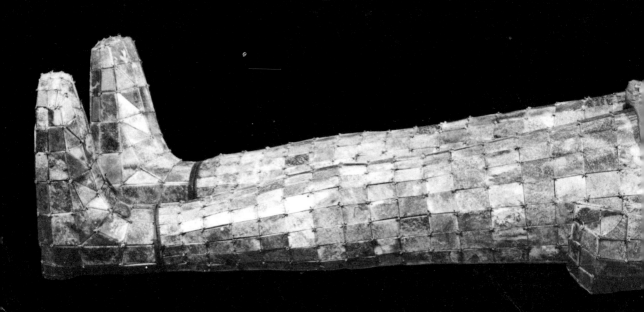

PRINCES
OF JADE

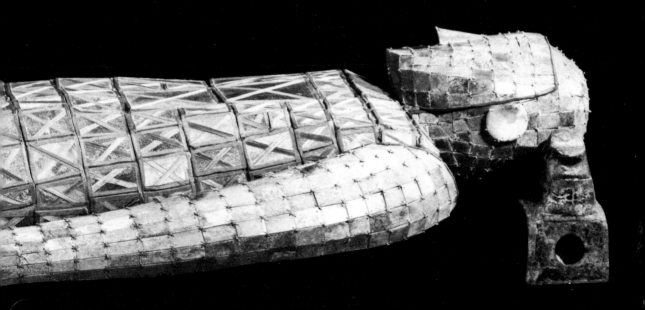

© Sphere Books 1973

Thomas Nelson and Sons Ltd
36 Park Street London W1Y 4DE
PO Box 18123 Nairobi Kenya
Thomas Nelson (Australia) Ltd
171–175 Bank Street South Melbourne
Victoria 3205 Australia
Thomas Nelson and Sons (Canada) Ltd
81 Curlew Drive Don Mills Ontario
Thomas Nelson (Nigeria) Ltd
PO Box 336 Apapa Lagos

First published 1973

Technical Data

Cameras: two Nikon F Photomic Tn, one Nikkormat FT

Lenses: Nikkor Auto 20 mm $f/3\cdot5$, 28 mm $f/3\cdot5$, 35 mm $f/2\cdot8$,
55 mm $f/3\cdot5$, 105 mm $f/2\cdot5$, 200 mm $f/4\cdot0$. All with
lens hoods and skylight filters

Film stock: Tri/X, Ektachrome-X and Kodachrome II given normal
exposure at meter readings with shutter speeds of
1/125th of a second or faster

Flash: three lightweight Mecablitz with mains charging units

Designed by Craig Dodd

Maps and Line Drawings by Derek Dooley

ISBN 0 17 141051 3

Printed in Great Britain by Jarrold and Sons Ltd, Norwich

*Right : Bronze finial in the form of an elk. Hsiung-nu art from the Ordos
regions, circa fifth century BC*

CONTENTS

Prince Liu Sheng

Princess Tou Wan

1 PRINCE OF HAN

LOOKING OUT ACROSS THE FLAT FERTILE PLAINS OF THE WEI RIVER, from the heights of the seventh-century White Goose Pagoda on the western outskirts of the city of Sian, towards the mountains which then rise continuously up to the far distant wastes of Central Asia, the smooth outline of the fields is punctuated by small abrupt mounds. These, we are told, are the tombs of members of the Imperial families of ancient China, of T'ang emperors, empresses and princes; as yet unexcavated, but surely housing a wealth of riches. It is ironic that, with all these known hoards of still buried treasure, one of the most stunning archaeological finds ever to have been made in China should have come about by accident.

In June 1968, a detachment of the People's Liberation Army was operating on a rocky limestone cliff on the Ling mountain, *Lingshan*, near the city of Man-ch'eng in Hopei province. The first indication of something unusual was the discovery of sections of a brick facing set deep into the rock. Sensing the significance of their discovery, the soldiers immediately reported to the authorities and soon representatives of the Institute of Archaeology of the Chinese Academy of Sciences and members of the Archaeological Team of Hopei province were at the scene. With the assistance of the local populace and soldiers of the PLA, they soon began to dismantle the wall. It was noticed that the areas above and around it were covered with small, loose stone chippings; when the wall was eventually removed and the doors of the tomb opened, it soon became apparent that the chippings were left over from the excavation of a vast underground mausoleum. When similar rock chippings were found some hundred metres to the north of the tomb, investigation led to the discovery of the second tomb.

The excavators entered the first tomb by way of a narrow tunnel-like passage which gradually widened to nearly fourteen feet. Forcing their way through fallen rocks and rubble, they passed two side chambers lying to the north and south, before emerging into a great underground cavern. This main chamber of the tomb measured some 50 feet in length, 40 feet in width and over 25 feet in height. At the far end, through the gloom of centuries, could be seen the stone doorway to a rear chamber.

By this time it had become clear to the excavators and archaeologists that this was no ordinary discovery. Surely the secret of this amazing underground mausoleum must lie behind that door. Its opening proved to be no easy task, for after burial the massive stone slabs had been sealed with molten iron.

8

Previous page : Bronze figure of a cavalryman on horseback. From the hoard recovered from a tomb at Leitai in Kansu province in 1969. This is the type of cavalryman that fought against the Hsiung-nu. Eastern Han Dynasty

Top right : The discovery of the tomb of Prince Liu Sheng, showing workers dismantling the brick facing to the entrance of the tomb in the summer of 1968 Bottom right : Archaeologists sorting material in Prince Liu Sheng's tomb

But their work was rewarded when, here in the rear chamber of the first tomb, the excavators found a body encased in a remarkable jade burial suit. Although it was known from ancient histories that such suits were made for Han emperors and highest ranking members of the aristocracy, this was the first of its kind to be recovered. In the companion tomb, just to the north, a second burial suit was found.

The partially fragmented jade suits were barely recognisable as such, while the magnificent bronze vessels, other jades, silver, gold, lacquer, pottery and silks were nothing more than roughly piled mounds shrouded in dust, dirt and rock chippings. Only gradually, as the excavators carefully removed and classified the material, did the richness and variety of their unique discovery became apparent. Many of the bronze vessels bore inscriptions, and as these were read and translated so the picture was pieced together. Most of these inscriptions began with the characters for 'Chung-shan nei-fu . . .' – Chung-shan was a kingdom of the ancient Han Dynasty which comprised fourteen counties and some six hundred thousand people, situated to the south-west of Peking in the modern province of Hopei. Who but the king could have been buried with such awe-inspiring grandeur? Further investigations into the Han Dynasty records and histories revealed that on the *i-hai* day, 27 July 154 BC, the Emperor Ching decreed that, '. . . his Imperial Sons, Liu Tuan be established as King of Chiao-hsi and Liu Sheng as King of Chung-shan, and granted to the common people one step in noble rank.'

The jade suit lying collapsed on the floor of the first tomb was that of the King of Chung-shan, Prince Liu Sheng, a son of the Emperor Ching who ruled the Han Dynasty from his accession to the Imperial throne in 157 BC to his death in March 141 BC. Emperor Ching had thirteen sons, offspring of five of his concubines, and one of them, Liu Ch'e, subsequently became the Emperor Wu, one of the strongest and most dynamic rulers in the history of ancient China. The second suit belonged to Liu Sheng's consort, the Princess Tou Wan.

Ssu-ma Ch'ien, the Grand Historian of China, in his monumental *Shih Chi* (*Records of the Historian*), written at the time of Emperor Wu late in the second century BC, notes: 'All the sons of the Emperor Ching by his five concubines were enfeoffed as kings. Some fulfilled their duties living in peace and harmony with their kind and, whether their domains were large or small, acting as bastions to the Imperial house. But others overstepped

Right : The central chamber of Prince Liu Sheng's tomb viewed from the entrance hall. In the background is the doorway to the burial chamber

中山內府
銅鈁一閣
四升重十
工斤八兩
第一廿四
圭中郎梛
市雒陽

their positions, and little by little their power declined and faded away.'

By all accounts Prince Liu Sheng was one of the less dedicated sons, as the Grand Historian again records: 'Liu Sheng loved to drink and was very fond of women so that, with all his offspring and their families, his household numbered over one hundred and twenty persons. He was always criticising his elder brother, the King of Chao, saying "Although my brother is a king, he spends all his time doing the work of his own clerks and officials. A true king should pass his days listening to music and delighting himself with beautiful sights and sounds."' To this his brother, the King of Chao, retorted in no uncertain terms: 'The King of Chung-shan fritters away his days in sensual gratification instead of assisting the Son of Heaven to bring order to the common people. How can someone like that be called a "bastion of the throne"?' Perhaps Liu Sheng may be partially forgiven for his short-comings; his father the Emperor Ching was one of the dullest and least resourceful of the Han emperors, who indulged his petty personal feelings and allowed his likes and dislikes to guide him, often in the face of the advice of his officials and counsellors.

Of Liu Sheng's mother we know little. Her name was Madame Chia and she is recorded in the history of the Dynasty merely as one of the Emperor's concubines and bearer of two of his sons. The regard in which she was held by the Court hierarchy is illustrated in an incident which occurred while the Emperor was on an outing to one of his favourite hunting and leisure palaces, the Shang-lin park. Madame Chia had retired to the toilet when suddenly a wild boar rushed into the room. The Emperor signalled to Chih Tu (general of the Palace attendants) to do something, but he refused to move, whereupon the Emperor himself seized a weapon and was about to go to her aid. Chih Tu flung himself to the ground before the Emperor and said: 'If you lose one lady-in-waiting, we will bring you another! The Empire is full of women like Madame Chia. But what about Your Majesty? Though you think lightly of your own safety, what will become of the temples of your ancestors and of the Empress Dowager?'

All the grandeur and the luxury of the lives of Prince Liu Sheng and the Princess Tou Wan are reflected in these impressive tombs and their contents. Above all, the great chambers, hollowed painstakingly out of the hard rock, must have involved an immense labour force, possibly of thousands, in many months or even years of work. It has been estimated that using modern   13

Top left : A square bronze wine vessel, hu, *recovered from the tomb of Prince Liu Sheng. The inscription refers to the state of Chung-shan*

Bottom left : Drawing of an inscription

on a bronze vessel from the tomb of Prince Liu Sheng, which refers to its use in the palace of the state of Chung-shan. It was through such inscriptions that the identity of Liu Sheng was discovered

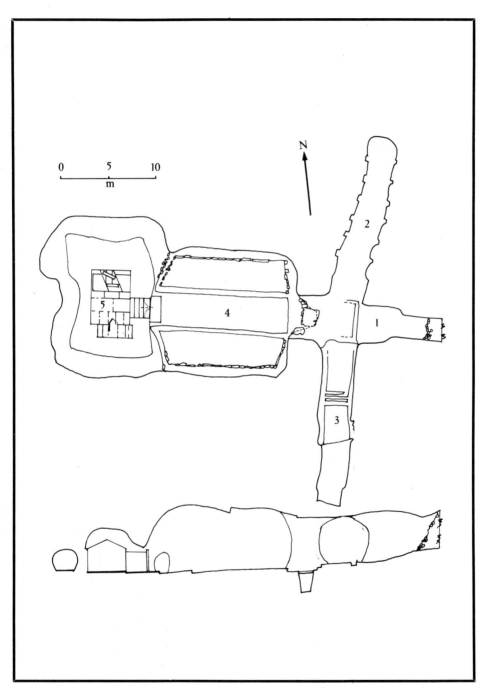

14

Plan and cross-section of the tomb of
Prince Liu Sheng

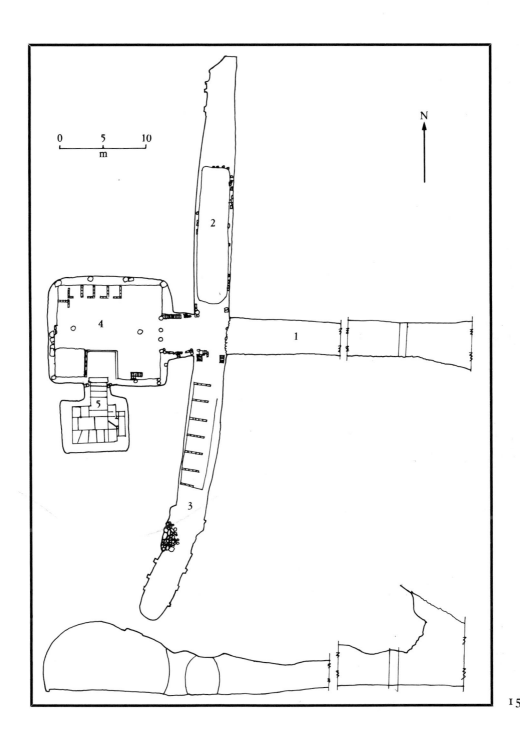

Plan and cross-section of the tomb of
Princess Tou Wan

techniques the construction of the two tombs would be a year's work for several hundred men.

The tombs are similar in shape, with entrance gallery, main chamber, rear chamber – which served as the actual burial room – and two long side halls, these running along a north-south axis. It is not difficult to imagine the funeral cortège of the Prince as it moved slowly and ceremoniously into the tunnel-like passage leading to the main chamber. He died in 113 BC, some years before the Princess Tou Wan, and no doubt his burial ceremonies were in accordance with the regulations contained in an edict issued by his father in 148 BC: 'When kings die, an Imperial Household Grandee shall be sent to condole, provide grave clothes, sacrificial food, funeral horses and carriages, oversee the mourning ceremonies and on the same occasion enthrone the son who succeeds to the kingdom.'

The funeral cortège of the King of Chung-shan must have been wheeled down into the mausoleum, for in the long and comparatively narrow (approximately twelve feet) southern extension chamber were found the remains of about a dozen horses and several chariots. Human sacrifice had been abolished, so that it was normal practice for the dead king to take with him into the tomb all those material things he might require in the after-life. Hence the horses and chariots to transport him, and in the northern extension chamber, hundreds of pottery vessels containing all manner of food and wine.

The grand central chambers of the two tombs contained vessels of less practical value but greater luxury; bronze urns and bowls, many inscribed with details of their use – for example, 'cup for use in the Chung-shan Palace', probably the King's own palace – lacquer wares and fine examples of pottery, much with painted decoration. These less mundane and utilitarian of objects were obviously considered more significant than those placed in the side chambers of the tombs. And yet there was more to come, for in the rear chambers, placed close to the bodies themselves, lay just a few objects of unsurpassed beauty and quality.

The body of Prince Liu Sheng was encased in a stone slab structure, rather like a miniature building, and here the Chinese archaeologists also found the truly magnificent Poshan incense-burner. Standing only some ten inches high, it nevertheless radiates vitality; on the lower bowl is a bold swirling pattern, delicately inlaid with gold, while the upper portion represents a mountain. Among the undulating peaks hunters and animals, tigers

16

Right : Detail of the jade burial suit of Princess Tou Wan, showing the head and face mask

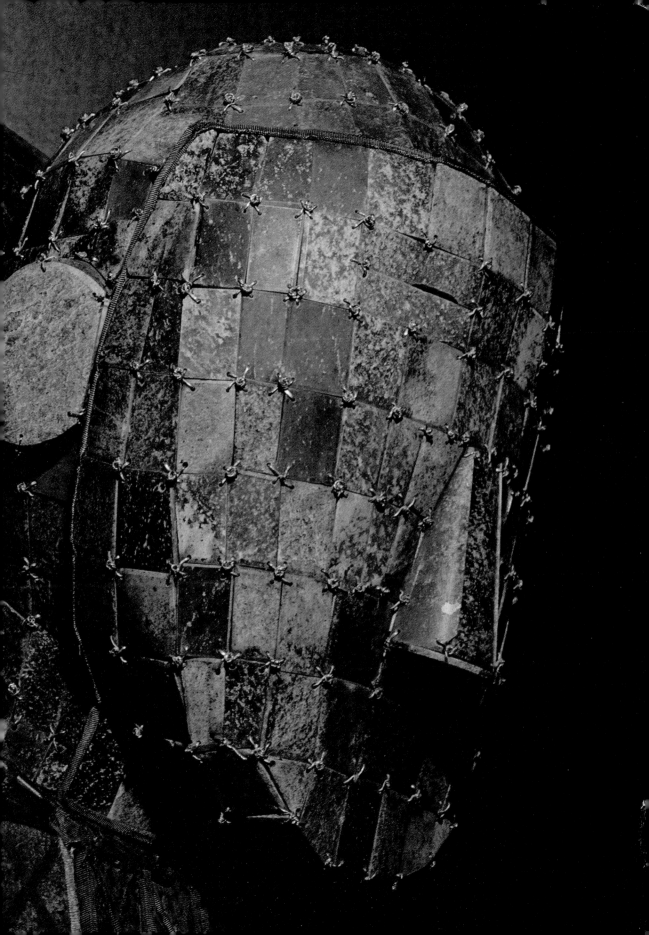

and deer, claw their way through the rugged terrain and peer anxiously from behind small peaks and hillocks. There are in Western museums a number of pottery and bronze examples of these incense-burners, but none of the quality and vivacity of this stunning find.

No less important in impact, originality and beauty is a magnificent and surprisingly large gilt-bronze lamp from the tomb of the Princess. The lamp, standing some nineteen inches high, is in the form of a kneeling girl, probably a palace servant, and in her hands she holds the lamp itself. The cylindrical form has sliding apertures so that both the direction and intensity of the light can be controlled. The smoke passes through the right arm, serving as a kind of chimney, and into the hollow body, thus keeping the room smoke-free. Inscriptions on the lamp record dedications to *chang-hsin*: eternal fidelity, and to *yang-hsin*: pure fidelity.

Also from the tomb of Tou Wan came the much smaller, twin-cupped vessel with a phoenix as the centrepiece. This too is made of gilded bronze, with engraved detail features, inlaid green stones and a jade ring suspended from the beak. Some of the finest objects to come from these tombs were inlaid with gold and silver, a technique which had developed along with new   17

Left : Part of the jade burial suit of the Princess Tou Wan.
Above left : An incense-burner of bronze, inlaid with gold. The upper part, depicting a mountain, is perforated, allowing the incense smoke to be emitted.

From the tomb of Prince Liu Sheng
Above right : Bronze lamp – a smaller version of the example in the form of a servant girl – but with a similar adjustable aperture. From the tomb of Princess Tou Wan

decorative styles in the fourth century BC. One example of this is the round bronze *hu*, a wine vessel with bulbous body and sharply tapering neck, retrieved from the tomb of the Prince. It is inlaid in gold with a bold swirling design of partially abstracted dragons.

Prince Liu Sheng also took with him into the after-life remembrances of both his official duties and his leisure activities. The archaeologists found ceremonial knives and swords of the type used at great annual sacrifices, these too sometimes inlaid with gold and silver and fitted with gilt-bronze or jade handles and accessories, all beautifully worked with semi-naturalistic designs of animals. Perhaps to remind the Prince and Princess of their days spent happily hunting in the Shang-lin park were the exquisite miniature images of seated leopards. The bodies of these leopards were finished in rich gilding with the plain bronze surface reserved for the spots. In spite of their size – each one is about four inches long – these noble figures none the less express all the tensions and power associated with the leopard.

There were all manner of other objects placed in the tombs, reflecting the many aspects of their lives. Stone, pottery and bronze images of servants and slaves were left to attend to the needs of their former master and mistress.

18

Above left : Bronze wine vessel, hu, *inlaid with broad scrolling dragon motifs in gold and silver. From the tomb of Prince Liu Sheng*
Above right : Bronze wine vessel, hu, *inlaid with a fine scrolling design in* *gold and silver. From the tomb of Princess Tou Wan*
Right : A large pottery tomb figure of a kneeling lady, excavated from a tomb at Lin-tung, Shensi province. Ch'in Dynasty

In all, over 2,800 objects were recovered, including gilt-bronze table legs, bronze mirrors, weapons, handles possibly from lacquered wood chests, woven and embroidered silks, painted lacquer bowls and of course, jades.

Once encased in their amazing jade suits, the bodies of the Prince and Princess were laid in their respective chambers, lying on their backs, the heads resting on fine gilt-bronze rests ornamented with animal heads and inlaid with jade. Placed close to the hands were flat, crescent-shaped jades, an unfamiliar shape whose function and symbolism is not known. Perhaps they are emblems of their status or office. It had, for example, long been the practice for enfeoffed kings such as Prince Liu Sheng to receive a jade as the token or emblem of that enfeoffment. In the ancient *Book of Documents*, a collection of announcements, counsels and speeches said to have been made from the very earliest periods in Chinese history, we read that the pre-historical period Emperor Shun performed a sacrifice, 'to the Lord on High, made pure offerings to the Six Honoured Ones [the four seasons, cold and heat, the sun, the moon, the stars and drought], sacrificed from afar to the mountains and rivers, and performed his obeisances to all the various spirits. Gathering together the jade tokens of enfeoffment from the five ranks of feudal nobles. . . .'

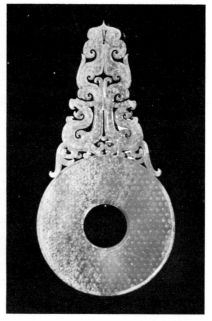

Above left : Ritual vessel, tsung, of green-brown mottled jade. Vessels of this type, thought to be symbolic of the Earth, were also found in the Man-ch'eng tombs. This is an earlier example, dating from the mid-Chou period, ninth–seventh centuries BC
Above right : Astronomical disc, pi, of white jade, the surface of which is orna-mented with granulated patterns and surmounted by a pair of dragons. From the tomb of Prince Liu Sheng

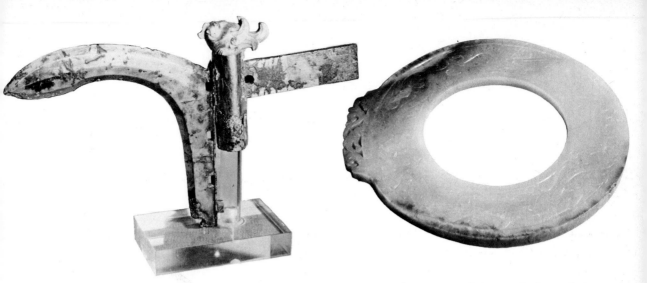

Because of its extreme hardness, its enduring qualities and the subtle beauties of the variable colourings, jade acquired a special place in Chinese art and mythology. It thus symbolised both power and virtue, and became the material for much sacrificial and ceremonial equipment. At the winter prayers and sacrifices made to recompense the gods for their favour during the year, 'a cow and a calf were invariably used as sacrifices, but the sacrificial implements and the offerings of jade and silk differed with the time and place'. Again when the Emperor Wu performed the sacrifice to the Great Unity, Ssu-ma Ch'ien records, 'The Supreme Emperor has for the first time performed the suburban sacrifice to the Great Unity at Yün-yang. The officials presented large armlets of jade and offerings of the finest sacrificial animals. On the night of the sacrifice a beautiful light appeared, and the following day yellow exhalations rose from the altar and reached to heaven.'

The 'large circlet of jade' referred to would have been what is termed a *pi*, the symbol of heaven. From the tomb of the King of Chung-shan came one of the most beautiful examples of a Han jade *pi*; the flat surface was finished with a granulated pattern and the ring surmounted with a dramatically carved dragon and phoenix, traditionally the symbols of the Emperor and Empress respectively. Other jades recovered from the tombs, nearly all coming from the actual burial chambers themselves, lend emphasis to the importance of jade in Chinese ceremony and the regard in which it was held. Mostly these other jades were ceremonial objects, such as the *pi*, either ornamental examples such as that described or plain simple discs, *tsung* vessels, symbols of the earth, and of course ceremonial knives and swords of the type used in sacrifices.

21

Above left : Halberd-head, ko, *of bronze with gilt bronze bird ornament From the tomb of Prince Liu Sheng*

Above right : Astronomical disc, pi, *of grey-green jade with brown markings, decorated with the animals of the four quarters. This is similar to the jade discs recovered from the tombs at Man-ch'eng. Western Han Dynasty*

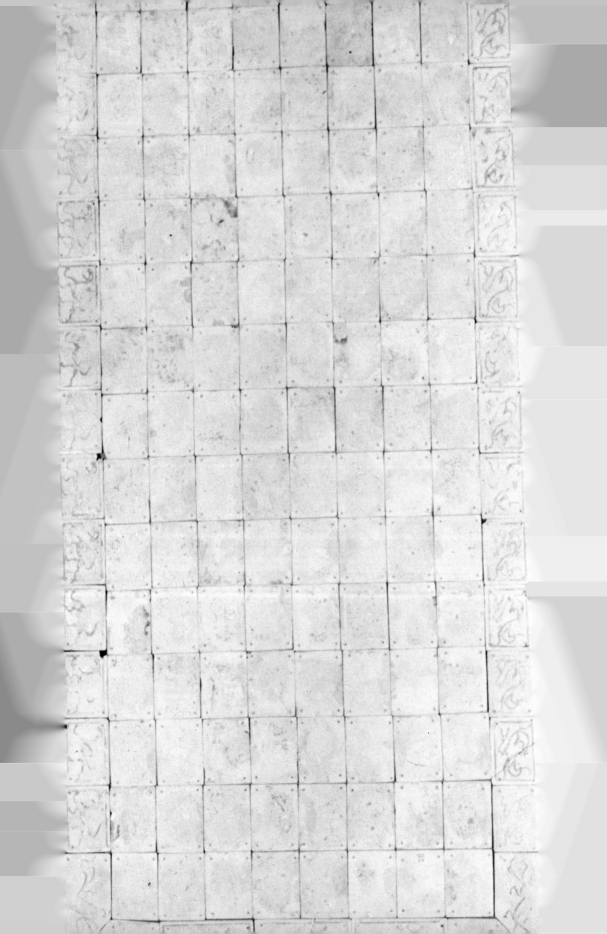

But the jade suits themselves outshine the other finds and embody all the mystical, magical and virtuous powers and qualities associated with the material. Merely as works of craft they are remarkable. Liu Sheng's suit was made from no less than 2,690 pieces of jade, the smallest measuring 1·5 × 1·0 cm and the largest 4·5 × 3·5 cm. Each piece was precisely carved and delicately finished so that when sewn together the whole suit would be both close fitting and flexible. The thickness of the jade varied between 0.2 cm and 0.35 cm.

The suit was made in sections, twelve in all, before fitting around the corpse. The small jade pieces were drilled with four small holes at each corner, so that they could be sewn together with gold thread. In their analysis of the suit of the Prince, Chinese archaeologists have calculated that 1,110 grammes of thread were used to sew the 2,690 pieces together. Even the thread was of the finest quality, some being made of no less than twelve fine gold strands. The suit of the Princess Tou Wan was similar both in construction and technique, but used fewer pieces, 2,156 in total, and just 703 grammes of gold thread. There was an interval of some years between the deaths of the Prince and Princess, and while the precise date of the Princess's death is not known, it seems unlikely that the suits are exactly contemporary with one another.

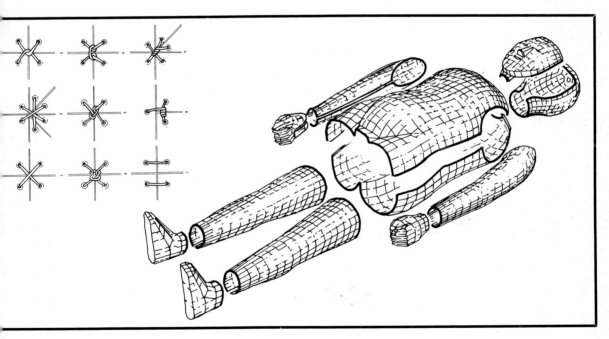

Left : Part of what was probably a burial suit similar to those of Prince Liu Sheng and Princess Tou Wan. In this example the incised designs were originally inlaid with gold

Above : The construction of the suits : the twelve sections were made independently and subsequently sewn together. This diagram also shows the various types of knots used in sewing together the jade pieces

As the Prince died first, in accordance with the very precise rules and regulations governing the burial rites of the upper echelons of Han society, the Princess's burial suit and funerary objects had to follow the pattern of those of her husband. It could be, of course, that the suits were made by the same hand or workshop, for it has been estimated that it would have taken an expert jadesmith of the Han Dynasty, using the tools and techniques known to have been available at the time, no less than ten years to make just one such suit.

It is, therefore, little wonder that the interest and excitement in the Western world caused by these extraordinary discoveries was matched, and perhaps promoted and stimulated, by the Chinese people's interest, and pride, in their cultural heritage. The first report of the find in the principal Chinese newspaper, the *People's Daily*, caused tremendous excitement, and the subsequent exhibition in the ancient halls of the Forbidden City in Peking was attended daily by throngs of visitors from all parts of the far-flung People's Republic.

A bronze lamp held aloft by a kneeling servant, from Prince Liu Sheng's tomb

2 CHINA BEFORE THE HAN DYNASTY

SOME FORTY-EIGHT KILOMETRES TO THE SOUTH-WEST OF PEKING near the small town of Choukoutien, lie the caves and crevices of the limestone Dragon Bone Hill. Here were discovered the remnants of a type of ancient man, known as the Peking Man. In 1929, when the first finds were made, it was thought that these were possibly evidence of the earliest man then known to the world, for they were datable to the Palaeolithic Age and were some four to five hundred thousand years old. Then, in 1959, in the Lantien district of Shensi province, Chinese archaeologists found the remains of yet another Palaeolithic ape-man, christened Lantien Man, and estimated to be five to six hundred thousand years old.

Both Peking and Lantien Man had a brain only two-thirds the size of their modern successor. They lived in caves, used the crudest of stone implements, and fed off the meat of the horses, antelope, deer and small animals which roamed the rich grasslands to the south. At the same time they had to defend themselves against the fearsome sabre-tooth tigers, boars, rhinoceri and elephants which lived among the forests on rolling hills to the north. Bears, hyenas and badgers shared the caves with these earliest known Chinese men.

Further up the Dragon Bone Hill, archaeologists have discovered the remains of a more advanced man, who lived ten to twenty thousand years ago. By then man was organising himself into recognisable social units, and developing manual skills. Perforated animal teeth, marine shells and stone beads found in these caves are probably the surviving remnants of the earliest jewellery in China.

Up to this time neither the habitat nor the mode of living of primitive man in China differed substantially from that of his Western fellows. However, in succeeding centuries, as an independent culture entered its earliest stage of development, certain distinctive characteristics emerged. Nearly all our knowledge of the nature of this society is based on later literary material and the facts inevitably lie buried beneath clouds of myth and legend.

The earliest ruler in China is recorded as having ruled from a date corresponding to 2852 BC, which must approximate to the formative years of the Neolithic era. The earliest figures in Chinese legend, after Pan Ku had 'chiselled' out the Universe, are the twelve Emperors of the Universe, the eleven Emperors of the Earth, each of whom reigned for a term of eighteen thousand years, and the nine Emperors of Mankind who reigned for a total of forty-five thousand years. These totally mythical figures were followed by

Previous page : Bronze tapir with surface decoration in Li-yü style. A small indentation on the back of the animal indicates that it was probably intended for use as a stand. Chou Dynasty, sixth–fifth centuries BC

Right : Portrait of the legendary Emperor, Shen Nung. A drawing from the San-ts'ai t'u-hui *(1609 edition)*

炎帝神農氏

27

the Three Sovereigns and the Five Rulers, all of whom may conceivably have been real historical figures.

Fu Hsi, reputedly with a dragon's body and a man's head, is generally placed at the head of the Three Sovereigns. His birth was as miraculous as his appearance; he was conceived through his mother stepping in the footprint of a giant. However, he is credited with some notable achievements, among them the invention of the Eight Trigrams – a set of diagrams which figuratively describe the evolution and cycles of nature – the use of nets for fishing and a number of useful crafts. To his successor, Shen Nung, is ascribed the invention of the hoe and the plough; in addition he taught the people the arts of farming, trade and medicine. Like Fu Hsi, he too was of miraculous birth, for he was conceived through the influence of a heavenly dragon upon his mother, the Princess An-teng.

Outstanding among the Five Rulers is Huang Ti, which means 'Yellow Emperor'. Ssu-ma Ch'ien, the earliest recognised historian in China (second century BC), acknowledges Huang Ti as the founder of Chinese civilisation, and the Emperor from whom all subsequent rulers and kings claimed descent. His list of achievements is endless. He is recorded as having invented wheeled vehicles, armour, ships and pottery, as well as drawing up regulations concerning religious ceremonies and sacrifices. Together with the other four of the Five Rulers, Huang Ti established a framework of crafts, ethics and government which was adopted by the later Confucian philosophers and thus became totally absorbed into Chinese civilisation. Of course the facts are disputable and it is well known that, in order to establish their priorities

28

Above left : Detail of a bronze ritual vessel, ts'un, showing a ram's head. Shang Dynasty, twelfth–eleventh centuries BC
Above right : Pottery funerary urn painted with zoomorphic designs, Pan-
shan type from Kansu province. Neolithic period, circa 2000 BC
Right : Portrait of the legendary Huang Ti, the Yellow Emperor. Drawing from the San-ts'ai t'u-hui (1609 edition)

黃帝軒轅氏

(and to strengthen their own foundations) the Confucianists created much of this legend and achievement. Two of Huang Ti's successors, Yao and Shun, are often known as 'model Emperors'. We are told that their conduct in all respects was beyond reproach and that they reigned during a golden age of perfect government. Indeed Shun, through his devout loyalty to his parents when admittedly not the favourite son, gained a place among the twenty-four examples of filial piety.

These Five Rulers did not found a dynasty, owing to the unworthiness of their sons and heirs. Thus it became the responsibility of the reigning Emperor to choose his successor. Shun selected Yü, because he had stemmed a terrible flood, a task in which his father had failed. The theme of the flood recurs again and again in Chinese history, and stories concerning the controlling of the great rivers, like the Yellow River in the north and the Yangtze to the south, are the inspiration of much legend, myth and heroism in Chinese literature. The terrible flood which Yü stemmed was probably caused by the Yellow River, for the ancient texts which record this early history are dotted with references to places in the Yellow River basin; the modern provinces of Honan, Shansi, Hopei and Shantung. Excavations of later archaeological sites confirm this area as the cradle of Chinese civilisation.

It is related that during thirteen years' epic work in controlling the rivers of China, Yü did not once enter his own house even though, on three occasions, he passed the door and heard the cries of his children. For such dedication he was selected as Ruler and founded the first dynasty, the Hsia. Although he nominated his minister as successor, the people insisted on recognising his

Above left : A water buffalo, carved from white limestone. Shang Dynasty, thirteenth–twelfth centuries BC
Above right : Bronze ritual vessel in the form of a bull with a tiger surmounting the lid. Western Chou period,
tenth century BC
Right : Detail of a rectangular bronze ting, *ritual food vessel, ornamented with a human face. Excavated at Ning-hsiang in Hunan province. Shang Dynasty, eleventh century BC*

son as Emperor, thus the lineage of a dynasty was established. Chieh, the last ruler, was a rogue and a tyrant whose cruelty became a legend. So tyrannical was he that one of his own nobles, T'ang, raised a rebellion, dethroned him, and established the Yin, or Shang, Dynasty (*circa* 1500–1027 BC). In accordance with the already established doctrine, T'ang claimed he was a descendant of Huang Ti, the Yellow Emperor.

Fortunately our knowledge of the Neolithic period in China (*circa* 2500–1500 BC) is greatly assisted by extensive archaeological remains. The picture which emerges from this material illustrates again the importance of the Yellow River basin, for it is here that the principal excavations have taken place and produced evidence of a painted pottery culture, termed 'Yang-shao', of considerable sophistication. On the outskirts of the modern city of Sian, capital of Shensi province, Chinese archaeologists have unearthed a Neolithic village at Pan P'o. The way in which the small circular houses tend to cluster round a larger rectangular building at this site suggests the existence of some form of local hierarchy. In turn, the smaller villages appear to have been centred around larger communities, suggesting that they were not totally independent.

Although the utensils and tools of Neolithic China were fundamentally the same as those of the Late Stone Age, if somewhat finer in finish, certain aspects of this culture display considerable advances. For alongside stone hoes and knives, stone spear- and arrow-heads, were discovered pottery vessels, with burnished surfaces and painted with highly developed, almost abstracted decorative motifs. It seems quite possible that these painted wares, so much more sophisticated and advanced than the day-to-day goods and materials of Neolithic man, were intended for some kind of ritual or sacrificial use. We have already seen, in the contents of Liu Sheng's tomb of over fifteen centuries later, the concern and wealth which were expended on ritual and sacrificial paraphernalia, and there is every reason to suppose that the tradition existed as early as the Neolithic period. Certainly there is evidence to suggest that ancestor worship, which would have required such material in the execution of ritual, was the principal religious activity, along with the usual earth, sun and rain worshipping philosophies.

Neolithic society in China also features two extensions, respectively in the west and east. In the west the culture, known as Pan-shan, is centred in Kansu province, bordering Central Asia, and displays certain influences

Right : Face of a servant girl from a gilt-bronze lamp ; the Han craftsman has here achieved supreme compassion, beauty and severity. From the tomb of the Princess Tou Wan

which may be ascribed to early Western and Near Eastern cultures. Again characterised by painted pottery wares, the distinctive large, ovoid funerary vases are quite unlike anything found in central China. Similarly the extravagant and lively zoomorphic designs have no counterpart in the central Yang-shao culture.

To the east of the Central Plain, in the coastal province of Shantung, archaeologists have uncovered the Lung-shan Neolithic culture. Again characterised by a distinctive pottery, in this case a burnished black ware, the Lung-shan culture appears to have moved westwards, for in the Central Plain it supersedes the Yang-shao material. Alternatively there is a suggestion that Lung-shan developed out of Yang-shao, in spite of the immense stylistic differences in their pottery wares. This theory seems somewhat contrived and maybe is wishful thinking on the part of those Chinese who seek to establish the Yellow River basin as the fount of Chinese civilisation. Whatever the movements in the Neolithic cultures, it is certain that in the Central Plain, the Lung-shan cultural remains overlay the Yang-shao and both in turn lie immediately beneath those of the succeeding Shang Dynasty. Thus a certain chronology is established.

A critical point in early Chinese history occurred with the establishment of the Shang Dynasty (*circa* 1500 BC) and the beginning of the Bronze Age. From this point on we can closely follow the development of Chinese culture, society and civilisation and see how the foundations of Han society were laid. Above all Shang society, on the evidence of archaeological remains, seems to have been based on a unified culture born out of the cross-currents existing between central Neolithic cultures, the Yang-shao and Lung-shan, and those of the south, far west and far north.

The Shang is characterised by the immensely sophisticated and technically accomplished bronze ritual vessels which may be seen in many Western museums. Large-scale excavations and pillagings of the vast royal tombs at the Shang capitals of Cheng-chou and Anyang, both in Honan province, have produced an impressive range of bronze vessels and weapons. These two cities formed the nuclei of a 'city state' in which the old Neolithic order of small villages clustering around a larger unit was enlarged to encompass the whole state, one which now occupied the Yellow and Yangtze River basins.

The Shang Empire was divided into nine provinces, each of which paid

33

Left : Gilt-bronze figure of a servant
girl holding the 'eternal fidelity' lamp,
from the tomb of the Princess Tou Wan

tribute to the emperor seated in the capital city. The extent of the Shang state must have made really effective political control difficult, and it seems probable that, in spite of the tribute paid, these provinces exercised a good deal of autonomy. However, Shang cultural remains tell a different story, for the bronzes and other artefacts display a similarity and consistency which would indicate a degree of unity and centralisation. Moreover the material indicates a totally independent culture: no other ancient bronze culture has produced such a range of exotic and individual vessels. The impressive and forceful monster masks, *t'ao-t'ieh*, which decorate most of the bronzes may have their origins in a wood-carving tradition, possibly from South China, although the concept of distorted two-dimensional representation existed in the Neolithic painted pottery bowls from Pan P'o village.

The practice of vast and impressive burials which was so characteristic of early China certainly flourished in the Shang. The tombs of the Shang kings were huge pits, entered by sloping roadways down which the chariots, horses and often slaves and servants were run. Such extravagances reflect their life on earth, where the Shang kings and princes lived in palaces and pavilions of great splendour, probably not dissimilar to those of the Han and succeeding dynasties. Stone was not generally used and the basic structure, a series of pillars, was always of wood. The walls, originally of pounded earth and later,

34

Above left : Bronze belt-hook designed around a dragon being attacked by four tigers. Third century BC
Above right : Bronze ritual wine vessel, yu. Early Chou Dynasty, tenth century BC

Right : Bronze axe-head surmounted by a human face : dating from the Late Shang period, eleventh century BC
Far right : Bronze axle-cap and linch-pin surmounted by a tiger's head. Mid-Chou period, seventh century BC

clay bricks, were usually little more than screens as protection against the elements and not in any way structural.

Whilst the Imperial household and the aristocracy lived in comparative luxury, the common folk lived in crude mud and straw huts substantially the same as those of the Neolithic period. The enormous distinction between the rulers and the ruled is highlighted by the sacrifices of human beings, usually in multiples of ten. In addition, the burial of the living with the dead further illustrates the tremendous social and economic cleavages in Shang society.

China was then, and still is, primarily an agricultural society. The vast mass of people was engaged in work on the land and still used primitive tools such as wooden ploughs and stone hoes. As in any early society myths, legends and associated rites grew up around the land, rain and the sun, and annual sacrifices were made to the grain crop, the soil and fertility. The other principal ideology in Shang China was based on ancestor worship. Even in Neolithic times it appears that the family rather than the individual, the state or the church was the most significant unit in society. Certainly this was the case in the Shang period. The establishment of ancestor worship as the focus of religious activities for the individual led to the development of certain characteristic social attitudes which were to become fundamental to Chinese society. The authoritarian, strictly hierarchic, nature of the family became so instilled into the Chinese way of life that it lasted, in principle, until the fall of the Dynastic era in 1911, and beyond. Indeed the whole structure of Chinese society, with power and authority emanating from the emperor, encouraged and maintained the institution.

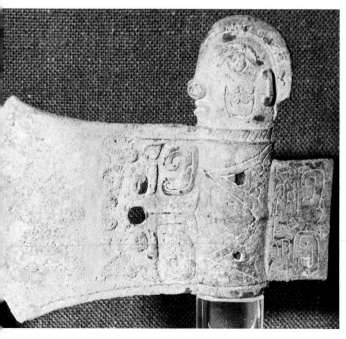

To the west of Shang territory, in the dramatic loess hills of the Wei River Valley in Shensi, lived the Chou people. Like the Shang they maintained a bronze culture, centred on their capital at Hao, near the modern city of Sian. This area adjoined Shang territory and there were clear cultural associations between the two; for example they seem to have had the same language and writing; and the bronze ritual vessels, also characteristic of Early Chou art, employed many of the same shapes, designs and decorative motifs. But the Chou people were closer to the 'barbarian' regions of the far west and far north and almost certainly maintained contacts with the nomadic sheep-herding tribes of Kansu and present-day Inner Mongolia – a relationship which may be responsible for the often less sophisticated but more exotic decoration of Early Chou bronzes.

This less restrained expression led to the traditional Chinese view that the Chou were a barbarian people who were 'civilised' by their inheritance of Shang culture, an opinion which is no longer entirely tenable in view of the quality and technical achievement shown in the earliest Chou bronze vessels. In any case, when the Chou finally defeated the Shang in 1027 BC, there was no sharp break in the emerging culture of China. They adopted the title of 'Wang' for their kings, followed the same ancestor-worshipping ritual, and practised similar rites in connection with nature and agriculture.

As with any conquering and invading power, the maintenance of order was a primary concern for the Chou rulers. Their problem was aggravated in an age of slow communications by the fact that the capital remained sited in Shensi in the north-west, while their territories now extended to the eastern seaboard. The Chou solution was a basically feudal system of government. Vassal kings, with delegated authority, ruled over most of those territories in the Central Plain and eastern provinces which were formerly in the hands of the Shang, while the Chou maintained direct control over the Wei Valley, their homeland. Generally these vassal kings were relatives and descendants of the Chou royal family and they acted in much the same way as did Prince Liu Sheng some fourteen centuries later. Each kingdom centred round a walled city and controlled the surrounding villages from which the vassal king levied taxes and tribute, and raised his army. Although more or less autonomous, they acknowledged the suzerainty of the Chou, and here the importance of family ties must have been a factor in maintaining the link between the central authority and the governing provincial hierarchy.

36

Right : A bronze model of two wrestlers,
probably entertainers. Chou Dynasty,
fifth–fourth centuries BC

Like the Shang, Chou society was sharply divided between the rulers and the ruled. The latter again far outnumbered the former. The strongly hierarchical system of government and the feudal network merely preserved and encouraged this division. The situation is summarised by a quote from a source of the second century BC, the *Li Chi* or *Record of Rituals*: 'The ritual does not extend down to the common people; punishments do not extend up to the great officers.'

In 771 the Chou removed their capital to a site close to the modern city of Loyang, in Honan province, and thus into the central arena of Chinese civilisation. Clearly this was a move to cement their position as rulers of China and may indicate a realisation of trouble threatening. This was in fact the case, for the states ruled by the vassal lords became increasingly independent and powerful and subsequently coalesced into twelve factions. As tensions between them increased, over territorial rights, tribute or strength and size of armies, so internecine warfare grew. While this situation was developing the vassal kings, recognising the strength of their own position, naturally became less and less interested in maintaining allegiance to the central Chou authority. Payments of tribute to the Chou kings began to fall

37

off as their effective power declined. To add to the troubles of the central Chou Court, there was increasing contact and conflict with the 'barbarian' pastoral tribes, nomadic peoples roaming the steppe lands to the far north and west. As the Chinese expanded, they inevitably became involved with neighbouring peoples and the nomadic tribesmen, probably of Turkish stock, who were in no way prepared to adopt the passive attitude of the Chinese people to the Chou rulers. It was these conflicts which led to the first sections of the Great Wall being built in the fourth and third centuries BC.

By the fifth century BC, effective control over the Middle Kingdom by the Chou Court in Loyang had been forever lost. The inter-state warfare escalated to such an extent that between 481 and 221 BC China underwent a period of perpetual strife, known as the Warring States period. The scale of the battles increased and it became common for states to field several thousand chariots, each accompanied by twenty or so peasant foot soldiers. More and more vassal warlords made demands on their peasantry as the armies grew in size to number tens of thousands. It was indeed a Dark Age for China, although one which has subsequently been immortalised in romantic and heroic accounts of battles and deeds of great courage.

Brittle alliances were negotiated, often temporarily strengthened through inter-state marriages of royal houses, but none succeeded. Gradually, however, one state began to take ascendance. Whilst states in the centre and south of China were busy engaging one another in total warfare and thereby eliminating themselves from the ultimate contest, the state of Ch'in, holding comparatively small territories in the west, prepared herself for expansion. In the late fourth century, moving out from her capital in the Wei Valley – where previously the Chou had risen to power – Ch'in captured the 'semi-barbaric' states of Shu and Pa in southern Szechwan. In 256 she calmly extinguished the Chou and embarked upon a series of immense campaigns which culminated in total victory in 221 BC. One of the great advantages of the Wei Valley for the Ch'in, as it was earlier for the Chou, was that this mountainous valley was accessible only through a gap between river and hills at the great bend in the Yellow River. Defence was thus far less of a problem than for her adversaries on the great plain.

Thus China was, for the first time, unified and so opened a new age in Chinese history; a fitting preface to the Han Dynasty.

38

Right : Detail of the animal mask on the handle of a large bronze ritual wine vessel, hu. *Chou Dynasty, eighth–seventh centuries BC*

The founding Emperor of Ch'in, Shih Huang-ti (literally, first Emperor) wrought dramatic changes in Chinese society. More than anyone he appreciated the need for a strong centralised authority to reconstruct an Empire which had disintegrated during three centuries of internal conflict. But he faced the same problems as the early rulers of Chou: vast distances, poor communications, difficult terrain and vestiges of feudal power among some of the surviving aristocratic families. However, he was equal to the task.

Shih Huang-ti recognised the absolute necessity to reform the power structure. Instead of parcelling out his conquests among his family, relatives and the established aristocracy, as earlier rulers had done, he adopted a centralised system and appointed competent officials to the local units of government. China was divided into thirty-six, later forty-two, commanderies and these subdivided into prefectures. Each commandery had at its head a Civil Governor (*Shou*), Military Governor (*Chün wei*) and an Observer (*Chien-yü-shih*), the central government's representative, who often acted as arbitrator between the other two. Through such a system, using political appointments, the grand family hierarchical system was abolished and the Feudal Age in China terminated.

One of the characteristics of a feudal society is the dependence of the vassal lord upon a large private army. Just as Shih Huang-ti deprived them of their vast landholdings, so he deprived them of their soldiers and weapons. Theoretically the only armed force in China during the Ch'in period was the Imperial army. Not that Shih Huang-ti ignored military matters. With his original seat of power located in the Wei Valley, close to the 'barbaric' steppe lands, he was well aware of external threats to his Empire. He therefore decided to consolidate sections of the Great Wall, joining and expanding sections built during the Warring States period.

The Great Wall of China extends along fifteen hundred miles, providing positive defence, climbing and twisting through dramatic, often barren, mountains, from southern Kansu province to the coast to the east of Peking. Since that time, it has been rebuilt and modified, principally during the Ming period (1368–1644), when the Chinese once again alienated themselves almost totally from the outside world. Although varying in both height and width, the wall averages twenty-one feet in height and the roadway on top approximately eighteen feet in width, sufficient for five horses to ride abreast. From the parapets of the wall, along which were built some twenty-five thousand

Opposite: Bronze finial in the form of
a ram, an example of Hsiung-nu
influenced art from the Ordos regions.
Fifth–third centuries BC

watchtowers, foot soldiers could fire their crossbows, a weapon far superior to the compound bow used by the mounted nomads. The combination of the sophisticated Chinese crossbow and the Great Wall was certainly the principal stabilising force in the northern and western border territories during the Ch'in and Han Dynasties.

Shih Huang-ti did not confine his authoritarian, centralised governmental policies only to land and defence. He unified weights and measures, standardised coinage, and also unified the axle length of wagons. This latter move may seem a rather strange and pedantic example of authoritarianism, but we have already seen the crucial importance of communications. The roadways of ancient China were unpaved paths, often passing through the narrow mountain passes and gulleys, especially in the north-west, where the transportation of men and materials to the defences of the Great Wall was a chief concern. The ruts cut by the wagon wheels thus became rather like tram-lines, and should a wagon with a larger or shorter axle traverse the same route it would clearly have difficulty in keeping stable.

This is just one indication of the tremendous outburst of physical energy during the Ch'in period, reflecting the desire for unity and peace after centuries of internal conflict and destruction. The sheer devastation of the Warring States period caused people to turn away from philosophical and ethical problems which were so stimulated by the conflicts, to concern themselves only with the reconstruction of their country, their farm holdings and livelihoods. Thus the common folk of China readily accepted the authoritarian rule of Shih Huang-ti.

41

Such an attitude inevitably involved the reconsideration of much that had gone before, and traditional Chinese thought and literature were to feel the effects of Shih Huang-ti's rule. Ancient books such as the *Classic of Documents* and the *Classic of Songs*, the former containing historical and semi-historical documents of the Early Chou period and the latter love, ritual and political poems and songs, had no place in such a down-to-earth utilitarian atmosphere. All such literary material, praising outmoded institutions and the values and histories of princely, aristocratic and feudal houses was considered thoroughly undesirable. Thus it was that in 213 BC Li Ssu, the leading statesman of the day, ordered the literary inquisition known as the 'Burning of the Books'. Only those books of obvious value on divination, medicine, agriculture, technology, etc., were spared.

The central feature of Early Ch'in power and the principal reason for its immense and rapid success was the Emperor Shih Huang. The very nature of the society he created was dependent upon a strong, utterly reliable and confident figurehead. He was a man who exuded those qualities of straight-forward, no-nonsense, dealing in all aspects of his life. However the very reasons for Shih Huang-ti's success were also the causes of his Empire's demise. When he died, during one of his indefatigable journeys through the Empire, Li Ssu and the Chief Eunuch, Chao Kao, placed on the throne a young and inexperienced son, who adopted the title Erh-shih Huang-ti (second Emperor). The demise of the Shih Huang-ti and the rise of the eunuch Chao Kao resulted in the total loss of the kind of dominant uncom-promising leadership which the Ch'in system of government demanded. By 206 BC, the Ch'in had fallen.

The collapse of so apparently strong a power illustrates a problem that frequently beset Imperial China. So often dynasties were established under the rule of an active competent emperor, only to fall at the second or later hurdle, when his successors failed to maintain the standards originally set. The seat of power then invariably fell to the Court advisers, eunuchs, or perhaps a peripheral member of the Imperial family. The failure of the Ch'in may also in part be attributed to the sternness and severity of Shih Huang-ti's rule. Nevertheless the achievement of Shih Huang-ti cannot be denigrated, for it was he who overthrew a feudal society and established a system of government that was to remain substantially the same for many centuries,

until the Revolution in 1911.

3 MIND OVER MATTER: from Confucius to Lao Tzu

IF ONE WERE TO CHARACTERISE CHINESE HISTORY OVER THE PAST two thousand years in a single word, it would be 'Confucian'. No other individual in Chinese history has had such a profound and lasting effect. It is strange therefore that the man who had such an impact should have led such an apparently commonplace and undramatic life.

Confucius was born in 551 BC, at a time when China was entering the Warring States period; an era of turbulence, political instability and social unrest. It was just these conditions that provided the stimulus for the greatest age of Chinese thought. Geographical expansion, new cultural contacts and the growth of new institutional methods stirred men's imagination. The breakdown of order, failure of the feudal system and subsequent loss of faith in many traditional attitudes permitted complete freedom in thinking and practical experiment. The comparison with the golden age of the Greek philosophers, in both time and nature, is striking.

At the same time the continual disturbances throughout the Middle Kingdom stimulated a desire for unity, control and self-discipline; qualities which were certainly recognised as essential by the great thinkers and philosophers of the time. Consequently political, social and philosophical thinking in the Warring States period tended towards a concern for mankind and the nature of man. It was a time for realistic and humanistic thought. The fundamental questions that were considered at such length concerned not man as an individual, but man in society. Here as always, we encounter that characteristic feature of Chinese society; the subordination of the individual to the mass – a feature as pertinent today in China as it ever was.

The Chinese have always been traditionally minded, and despite the revolutionary thought of the Confucian and immediately post-Confucian era the dependence upon, and veneration for, ancient writings was as strong as ever. These earlier writings were generally considered to be classics by Confucius and his contemporaries, and included the *Classic of Songs* and *Classic of Documents*, already mentioned in connection with the infamous 'Burning of the Books', the renowned *I Ching (Classic of Changes)* a textbook of divination and the *Li Chi (Record of Rituals)*. This last book had a particular relevance in Confucian thought, for ritual was considered to be a vital part of the social order.

Confucius was born in the coastal province of Shantung, in the small feudal state of Lu. His family name was 'K'ung', and the name Confucius is

44

derived from the Latinised form of 'K'ung Fu-tzu', 'Master K'ung'. We are told that his parents were minor aristocrats, although by the time the Master was born, the ravages of the conflicts and disturbances had reduced them to poverty. Confucius' father died when he was very young, thus he was left to secure his own education and future. Somehow he managed to gain employment in government in his native state of Lu, but his political career seems to have been a failure and he turned to teaching. He travelled extensively, preaching his thoughts for the re-establishment of order and is reputed to have had some three thousand students at one time.

The profound and lasting influence of Confucian thought lay in the scope and depth of his thinking. First, he described a code of living based on moral principles but within a traditional Chinese framework, and second, this code **was** perfectly embodied in the patriarchal nature of the Chinese family. Above all Confucius was a great moralist, and his chief aim was to propagate his ethical principles so that they should become fundamental aspects of Chinese society. History shows that to a large extent he was successful. His teachings became established through the training of the official class; the *Chün-tzu*, which literally translated means 'ruler's son', but which generally became a term applied to well-educated and responsible officials, 'men of nobility'. These were the men who surrounded the Emperor and provincial rulers. Prince Liu Sheng himself, no doubt brought up according to the Confucian ideal, would have relied on such 'men of nobility' for the management of his affairs and land.

The Confucian ethical code was constructed round the 'virtues' which, it was said, the *Chün-tzu* should possess. These were *chih* (wisdom, integrity), *i* (righteousness), *chung* (conscientiousness and loyalty), *shu* (altruism) and the quality he considered most important of all, *jen* (love and human-heartedness). In addition the 'gentleman' was expected to have *wen*, meaning culture, and *li*, meaning literally ritual. In Confucian terms this meant an understanding and appreciation of proper decorum and etiquette.

Our knowledge of what Confucius thought and said about *jen* and the other virtues is obtained from the only work known to be by him, the *Analects* (*Lun-yü*), which consists largely of his answers to questions, each one prefaced by 'The master said . . .'. Although much of his ethical code reflects human nature, and thus by our standards perhaps man's inherent qualities, he insisted that all depended upon education: 'By nature men are pretty   45 much alike; it is learning and practice that set them apart.' Thus he distinguished his élite, the *Chün-tzu*. His insistence upon the vital importance of learning and the desire to learn is again illustrated in another quote from the *Analects*: 'Those who are born wise are the highest type of people; those who become wise through learning come next; those who learn by overcoming dullness come after that. Those who are dull but still won't learn are the lowest type of people.' We see here another characteristic of Confucius and his thinking – the tendency to categorise and his positive belief in the need for hierarchy.

Probably the fundamental Confucian virtue is *jen*, which may be translated as 'goodness', 'love', 'humanity'. When asked by a follower, Tzu Kung: 'Is there any one word that can serve as a principle for the conduct of life?' Confucius replied: 'Perhaps the word "reciprocity": do not do to others what you would not want others to do to you.' This could be accounted the nature not only of love and human-heartedness but also of *shu* (altruism).

An aspect of the virtue of *chung* (loyalty) which Confucius particularly emphasised was that of filial piety. Clearly he felt that this was a declining virtue, for when asked by Tzu Yu about filial piety, the Master replied: 'Nowadays a filial son is just a man who keeps his parents in food. But even dogs or horses are given food. If there is no feeling of reverence, wherein lies the difference?' The unity of the family was, as we have already seen, a dominant feature of early Chinese society. That it remained so for the next two thousand years is testimony to the strength of the Confucian ideal. Indeed, even in the modern People's Republic of China, the family unit although subjugated to the political and social aims of the country as a whole still remains a vital social force. In ancient society the ideal was to have all the living generations of a family inhabiting one large compound of houses and courtyards. Seldom achieved by the peasant farmers who had to make do with their mud and straw huts, although even they may well have had parents, grandparents and children under one roof, this was certainly how Prince Liu Sheng would have lived. Being of royal birth, his brothers would have had their own territories and palaces, but in their respective households would have resided any number of relatives and dependants.

We must also give brief consideration to the ancillary Confucian virtues of *wen* and *li*, for these two concepts were to become basic issues for the ruling
classes of Imperial China. *Wen* quite literally means culture, although it

47

Drawing taken from a painting of a
group of officials, in their long flowing
robes and official bonnets of the type
that the first Han Emperor, Kao Tsu,
found so offensive. From a Han tomb
in Honan province

inevitably took on a wider meaning. In contemporary terms it might be translated as 'polish', or 'sophistication'. Education played a vital role in the acquisition of *wen*, for it depended upon the study and understanding of the ancient classics – thus it became available only to those able to afford an education and willing to learn. *Li* is an aspect of the same quality, in that it concerns behaviour. It may be translated as 'rites', or 'ritual', and we know that Confucius placed great emphasis on the maintenance of ancient rituals. They were another method of establishing and expressing order and the hierarchy. But it was not just a matter of observing the intricacies of ceremony, for always in the forefront of Confucian thinking was the attitude of mind. When asked about the fundamental principle of rites he replied: 'You are asking an important question! In rites at large, it is always better to be too simple than too lavish. In funeral rites, it is more important to have the real sentiment of sorrow than minute attention to observances.' At another occasion he commented: 'Rites, rites! Does it mean no more than jades and silks? Music, music! Does it mean no more than bells and drums?'

It must again be stressed that these rules, conditions and standards propounded by Confucius and subsequently so much a part of traditional China applied only to that comparatively small section of the community, the ruling classes. And when we speak of traditional China, Confucian China, it is constituted by the society which surrounded the Emperor and his Court, the aristocracy, and the *Chün-tzu* – the mandarins. It was these people, who, like Prince Liu Sheng, wore the fine silk robes embroidered or brocaded with dragons, lived in palaces and pavilions with highly painted and lacquered timber, were attended by countless servants, and rode in chariots and carriages drawn by horses with lacquer and bronze trappings.

One of the great features of Confucianism is that, in spite of certain rigorous attitudes, it was a philosophy of compromise. Confucius recognised the importance of the external façade, particularly where the ruling classes were concerned, but at the same time never abated extolling the true virtues – the real inner qualities of men. Thus he had to strike a balance between these inner virtues and the external polish; the resultant relativity and moderation of thought is one of Confucianism's great attributes. It established the notion of what has subsequently been termed the 'Middle Path'. His great follower Mencius said: 'Confucius did not go to extremes.'

48 Mencius, who lived from *circa* 373 to 289 BC, is the best known of the

Right : The jade burial suit of the
Prince Liu Sheng, King of Chung-shan

Over : Full length view of the jade
burial suit of the Prince Liu Sheng

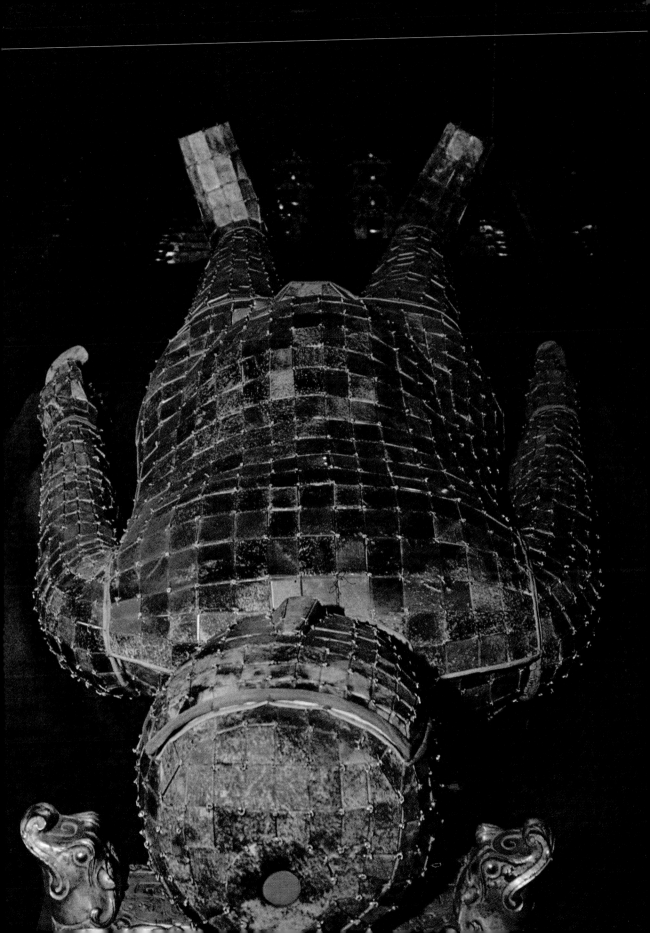

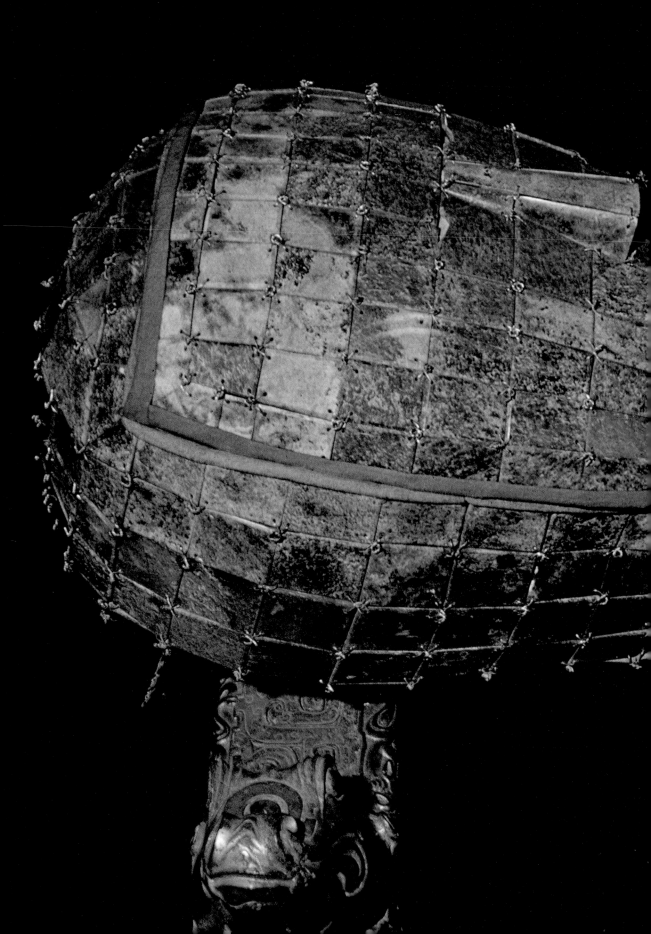

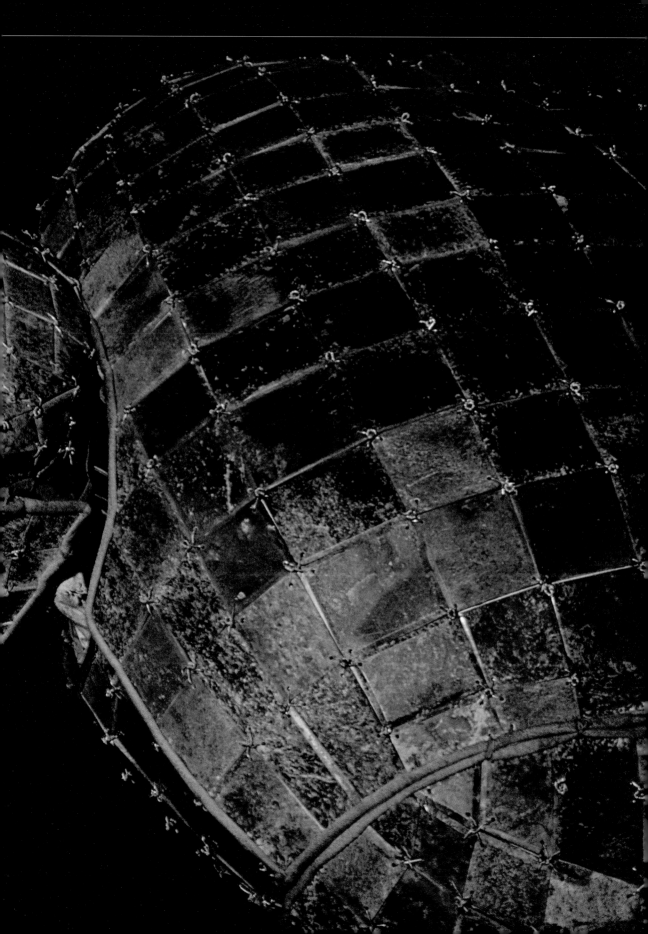

followers of Confucius. Yet as well as a follower and disciple, he was a philosopher in his own right. He was in many ways like Confucius, wandering from state to state seeking a suitable government post – and failing. And he too became something of a roaming philosopher, observer and talker – a champion of human rights. It is probable that he had a rather easier time than his predecessor, for by the fourth century BC, the role of the itinerant philosopher-statesman was much more revered than it had been some two centuries earlier.

Mencius' great contribution to Confucian thought, and indeed to basic philosophy, was his belief that all men are fundamentally good. Thus he immediately withdrew that distinction between aristocrat and peasant which had become so instituted into Chinese social life. Such an acknowledgement implied that entry to the official or *Chün-tzu* class was available to all, by the removal of that fundamental barrier which insisted that only those of aristocratic birth had the required moral and ethical potential. For Confucius, with his emphasis on teaching, education and the Classics, never permitted himself the luxury of admitting that all men were basically equal. Mencius' analogy with the natural flow of water illustrates the point: 'The tendency of human nature to do good is like that of water to flow downward. There is no man who does not tend to flow downward. But you may strike water and make it splash over your forehead, or you may even force it up the hills. But is this the *nature* of water?' Thus he believed that the most important of the Confucian virtues, that of *jen*, existed in all men, only the forces of circum-stances and environment – external factors – obstructed the expression of goodness.

Directly related to his views on *jen*, are Mencius' views on that other fundamental Confucian virtue *i*, or righteousness. Basically, Mencius con-sidered *i* to be merely the outward expression of *jen*. A conversation between the master and his follower, Kao Tzu, shows how he distinguished between the internal and external qualities of men:

Kao Tzu: The appetite for food and sex is part of our nature. Humanity comes from within and not from without, whereas righteousness comes from without and not from within.

Mencius: What do you mean when you say that humanity comes from within while righteousness comes from without?

Kao Tzu: When I see anyone who is old I regard him as old. This regard for age is not part of me. Just as when I see anyone who is white I regard him 49 as white, because I can observe the whiteness externally. For this reason I say righteousness comes from without.

Mencius: Granted there is no difference between regarding the white horse as white and the white man as white. But there is no difference between one's regard for age in an old horse and one's regard for age in an old man, is there? Moreover, is it old age itself or our respectful regard for old age which constitutes a point of righteousness?

Kao Tzu: My own brother I love; the brother of a man of Ch'in I do not love. Here the decision for the feeling depends entirely on me; thus it is internal [or humanity]. An old man of Ch'u I regard as old, just as an old man among my own people I regard as old. Here the decisive factor for the feeling is his old age, and thus it must be external [or righteousness].

Mencius: We love the Ch'in peoples' roast as much as we love our own. Here we have a similar situation with respect to things. Do you, therefore, say that the love of roast is also something external. . . .

As we can see, Kao, although a follower of Mencius, did not readily accept the premise that righteousness was directly related to inner goodness, and thus the principle that all men are inherently good. The important point of the conversation is that it illustrated Kao Tzu's failure to make, what Mencius felt, was a vital distinction: between the true nature of man and the nature of his feelings and reactions under given conditions or circumstances.

This excerpt also illustrates the nature of the discussions which occurred at the time: endless discourse on minute points of moral and ethical interest, highlighted by often quite arbitrary analogies, but which challenged and questioned the most fundamental, and generally accepted, tenets of social and philosophical thought. It was a time of complete re-evaluation which could perhaps be equated with more recent events in China, the Cultural Revolution of 1966–68.

In practical terms Mencius was even more insistent than Confucius that good government depended upon the humanitarian and ethical qualities of the ruler. Bearing in mind his recognition of that fundamental goodness in man, we can see that Mencius felt it of vital importance that the government – the ruler and his officials – display the highest moral standards and ideals in the execution of their duties. With a true and, for that time, somewhat revolutionary sense of social and political responsibility, he insisted that the governor existed for the sake of the governed – an idea that the feudal princes of Chou must have found quite extraordinary, and not at all to their liking. It was because of his championship of the common people that Mencius, and his surviving work (the *Mencius*, thought by many to have been written and compiled by his followers) were regarded as 'dangerous'.

In many ways Mencius, like Confucius two centuries earlier, was a man out of tune with his time. His intense idealism, however commendable, could not survive in an environment suffering from feudal conflicts. A rather more rational view of the Confucian order was taken by Hsün Tzu (*circa* 300–272 BC). Evidence of his more realistic approach is provided by the fact that he managed to obtain and hold down a position in government; he was high official in the states of Ch'i and Ch'u.

Hsün Tzu opposed the basic tenet of Mencius' thinking, that man is by nature good. He argued that man's inherent emotional and natural desires inevitably lead to conflict and are thus evil. The remedy for this, he said, lay in education. Strict, formal education was vitally important as it was this, and only this, which could teach mankind the restraint and discrimination needed to combat his basically evil nature. It is interesting that two followers of one philosopher could have such totally opposite ideas. And yet both were agreed upon the worth and attainability of perfect virtue, and both recognised the importance of education in this attainment. To Mencius goodness was inherent in man, to Hsün Tzu it was a hard-won achievement.

A consequence of Hsün Tzu's somewhat pessimistic view of life was his emphasis on formal education which 'begins with reciting the Classics and ends in learning *li*'. He was also probably influenced in the formation of his dogmatic approach and ideas by the growing interest in the supernatural in China at that time. To a man not given to idle, romantic thought, such beliefs, which were gaining much support from the common people, were both unsettling and irrelevant. It is also pertinent to remember that Hsün Tzu appeared relatively late in the period of great debate, and he could therefore look back and consider the arguments and conclusions of his predecessors, and their successes and failures. He opted for a tough Confucian line and the effect of his deliberations upon the government of the time was significant. We have already seen that the Ch'in government adopted an authoritarian, and yet basically Confucian, philosophy. The influence of Hsün Tzu is strongly evident here, as it is in the subsequent Han government, which again held rigidly to Confucian principles.

The appearance of the government was, perhaps, in Confucian terms as important as its substance. We have noted that he wrote at length about the virtue of *i* (righteousness), which was the external expression of *jen*. Similarly, he wrote at length about *li* (rites), the external expression of government and the hierarchy. Naturally *li* figures strongly in the writings of Hsün Tzu, where it is as difficult a term to interpret as any of the Confucian virtues and qualities. In addition to the primary meaning of 'rites', in varying contexts it can be translated to mean 'social behaviour' or 'decorum', as well as religious or social ceremony. Hsün uses the term *li* in both its general and individual senses. He says: 'Rites [*li*] rest on three bases: heaven and earth which are the source of all life; the ancestors, who are the source of the human race; sovereigns and teachers, who are the source of government.'

Of the first basis he says: 'It is through rites that Heaven and Earth are harmonious and the sun and moon bright, that the four seasons are ordered and the stars set on their courses, that the rivers flow and that nature rejuvenates, that love and hatred are tempered and joy and anger are in keeping. They cause the lowly to be obedient and the illustrious to be on high.'

Of the second basis he says: 'If there were no ancestors, where would the offspring come from?' Thus to 'honour the ancestors' was a practice vital to secure noble birth for the future.

Of the third basis he asks: 'If there were no sovereigns or teachers where would the government come from?' In honouring the sovereigns, teachers and sages in such a way, he was of course elevating them to a position beyond that of the ordinary mortal. This again is merely a reinterpretation, perhaps an exaggeration, of traditional Confucian thinking. But in practical terms it tended to widen the already tremendous gulf between the educated classes and mass of the people.

In Hsün Tzu we see a rigidly authoritarian and uncompromising interpretation of Confucianism. Displaying similar qualities, but within the framework of another version of Confucianism, is the philosophy of Mo Tzu (late fourth to early third centuries BC). His ideas lacked any sentiment and were totally utilitarian, devoted to the practical matters of government and the reconstruction of the Empire. Although Mencius considered him the most 'dangerous' of the Confucian philosophers, owing to his apparent lack of humanity and human considerations, it is only fair on Mo Tzu to remember that he lived in the middle of the Warring States period when continual warfare was ravaging the country.

Most offensive of all to the traditional Confucians was Mo's attitude to their beloved and esteemed ritual. To Mo, the great utilitarian, all such pageantry was wasteful, extravagant and in no way helpful in satisfying the needs of the people.

Satisfying the needs, the essentials, of the people was really the basic premise of Mo Tzu's whole philosophy. In pursuance of this he advocated the concept of universal love for, he felt, a love for all men was best shown by attending to their needs and abandoning all selfish enterprises which did not contribute towards feeding, housing and clothing the people. To the common people of the fourth century BC, all this was particularly relevant, but to the aristocracy and ruling nobles it must have been as revolutionary as the theory of inherent goodness in man proposed by Mencius.

Mo Tzu also lived by the exacting standards he set in his writings. Unlike the true Confucian who offered his advice only in advantageous circumstances and always bearing in mind the position of the ruler and the hierarchy beneath him, Mo offered his thoughts and advice to all who would listen. Not for him the fine silks, carriages and lacquered furniture of the traditional scholar/gentleman. Mo drove himself tirelessly in the prospect of universal love – it is recorded that when he heard of a state planning to make war, a common occurrence at that time, he would hasten to the seat of government and try to dissuade those in power from undertaking military action. War, he said, was every bit as evil as excessive ritual; both are wasteful of materials and a retreat from the aim of providing for all.

Universal love had little consideration in the philosophies offered by yet another group of social and political theoreticians, the Legalists. As their name implies, their views were rigidly authoritarian, supporting the type of hierarchy which existed in feudal China. Indeed it has been said that the Legalists' ideal state was one in which 'an uneducated citizenry would blindly follow and obey an all-powerful hierarchy'. But the Legalists were very much a product of their time. The anarchic conditions of the Warring States period could only be repaired by stringent law; a view, as we have seen, also shared by Hsün Tzu. The Legalists believed human nature to be thoroughly evil at heart – hardly a blameworthy observation at that time. They were also sufficiently realistic to appreciate that differing circumstances required differing methods of government.

Shang Yang (died 330 BC), Prime Minister of the state of Ch'in, is generally considered to be the founding father of the Legalist order, and its first historically important representative. However, it is to the third-century BC writer and political theoretician Han Fei-tzu that we must turn in order to obtain more precisely the views of the Legalists. Han was a student of that wayward Confucianist, Hsün Tzu, and a great friend of Li Ssu, the first Prime Minister of the strong-arm Ch'in Dynasty.

In brief, the Legalists rejected the traditional Confucian virtues of humanity (*jen*) and righteousness (*i*) as irrelevant niceties in a hard, tough world. They freely advocated war as a method of establishing law and order, and restraining and destroying elements of resistance to their ideal. The feudal system of dispersed political power was unacceptable to the Legalists, who strongly advocated the absolute authority of the monarch and the central government. The state would be subject to exhaustive laws setting out in detail the duties and responsibilities of all sections of society, and of course they insisted on a rigid hierarchy. Being of a practical nature, they intensively promoted agriculture as the foundation industry of China, and spared little time or energy for the affairs of the merchant, trader, intellectual or scholar.

The hard-headed down-to-earth philosophies expounded by the Legalists enjoyed some acceptance during the third century BC while China was in the final stages of the Warring States period. The initially immensely successful Ch'in government was basically Legalist. However, as we have seen, the uncompromising inflexibility of their rule betrayed those qualities of adaptability, symbolised by the bamboo which bends but never breaks, so characteristic of the Chinese people.

However diverse the various schools of thought, Confucian or Legalist, they were all concerned, if only in part, with the practicalities of governing and managing the country. There was, however, a third force in the ascendant at the time. Next to Confucianism, Taoism has been the most important and influential of native Chinese doctrines. It too was a product of the general rebellion against the conditions which prevailed, but instead of proposing order, law and strong government, Taoists championed the independence of the individual whose principal concern, they insisted, was to find his own place in society and nature. To them man-made society was an irrelevant contrivance bound to promote conflict among men.

The Taoists sought to attain a state of harmony with nature, and then with mankind, through the study and understanding of the *Tao*. Literally translated *Tao* means the 'road' or the 'way'. It was a term used by Confucius to describe his social system, but subsequently adopted, more appropriately, by the Taoists; to them it signified the pattern or form of nature. The basic Taoist text, the *Tao-te-ching* or *Lao Tzu*, probably dates from the third century BC, although it is traditionally attributed to the 'Old Master' himself, Lao Tzu. Like the other socio-philosophical works of the period, it proposes a system of social structure and government, but in place of the dry, pedantic gravity of Confucius, or the pompous authoritarianism of the Legalists, we have here a mystic, poetic and often witty solution to the problems of mankind, and Late Chou China in particular.

The whole philosophy of Taoism rests on the central principle of the *Tao* as the source and controller of all life, both human and natural, the fundamental force which resolves all the contradictions and distinctions of existence. Such notions enter into the world of metaphysics and involve problems concerning the nature of nature and the universe which even today are beyond our comprehension. The Taoists recognised this: 'The Tao that can be told of is not the eternal Tao. The name that can be named is not the eternal name. Nameless, it is the origin of heaven and earth. Named, it is the mother of all things.' Like all mystics, the Taoists found it difficult to express their ideas; indeed grasping and understanding such concepts was their principal problem. Only through meditation, they said, could such enlightenment be obtained. It was, however, a very distinctive meditation, based on

Right : A set of twelve pottery tomb figures depicting the animals of the Chinese zodiac : the rat, ox, tiger, hare, dragon, snake, horse, sheep, ape, cock, dog and wild-boar. Sixth century BC

the doctrine of *wu-wei*, or 'doing nothing'. This was a call not to total idleness but to acting and reacting naturally, unhampered by the conditions and standards of the environment. Such attitudes were in total opposition to the Confucian and Legalist ethics.

'Do nothing, and nothing will be undone', this was the maxim applied to the doctrine of *wu-wei*, for one action implies another. The Taoists totally accepted the constant movements of nature in a way which we today may regard as fatalistic. Nature and the universe will continue and it is the duty of man to adjust to that momentum, not to try to adjust the momentum itself. This belief in natural action, that things will occur spontaneously, was the way of life of Taoism. Man's efforts to interfere with the harmonies of nature would only produce chaos. Understanding, not knowledge, was the key to the Taoists' ideal state. The Confucian virtues merely heightened those qualities of which the hierarchy either approved or disapproved; the laws of the Legalists merely created crime. In the same way knowledge could only corrupt in that it created desire. Taoism was a sophisticated philosophy, promoting an almost primitive way of life.

One of the outstanding features of this era of the great philosophers in

China is the extraordinary diversity of thought, ranging from the romantic mysticism of the Taoists on the one hand to the strong arm of the realistic Legalists on the other, and in the middle the Confucian school – 'Confucius did not go to extremes' – variously interpreted from the humanitarian views of Mencius to the rather less compromising attitudes of Hsün Tzu. All these schools of thought achieved some success, some recognition but in the end it was the true 'middle of the road' Confucian school which won through.

4 THE HAN DYNASTY

THE FOUNDING OF THE HAN DYNASTY INAUGURATED A PERIOD
which, throughout its dynastic history, China has held in the highest esteem
as one of the great ages of its Imperial past. The Han grew out of turmoil, and
once again was established by a man of great and uncompromising strength.

This man, Liu Pang, came from humble peasant origins to become a
leader of one of the many rebel and bandit groups which emerged to challenge
the severe authority of Ch'in. We have seen how the Ch'in destroyed once
and for all the ancient feudal system of China, but dissatisfaction and
impatience with their rulers led these rebel bands to act and resist, often in the
name of one of the old royal houses. This claim may have given them respect-
ability in the eyes of the people, but in practice it was totally unrealistic to
attempt a revival of the old society. It is likely that many of these rebels had
no wish to re-establish a feudal empire. Their motives were clearly inspired
by the hard rule of Ch'in, and the prime objective was to destroy that order,
not to re-establish an old one.

Certainly the overthrow of Ch'in was uppermost in the mind of Liu Pang,
and the fact that many other aspects of ancient China also fell by the wayside
in the process was merely unfortunate, and to him largely irrelevant. Historians have recorded that the destruction of old institutions, ideas, literature
and philosophies by Liu Pang and his contemporaries in revolt was probably
as great, if not greater, than the destruction caused by the Ch'in. Liu Pang
in particular was a man of little education, not greatly inclined towards the
Classics or the Confucian ideal. According to one of his biographers Li Yi-
chi, his dislike for the Confucian scholar was intense. Some time before 207
BC, in the early part of his career as a general, Liu Pang was obliged to receive
some of these scholars, who arrived in the full regalia of the literati, bonnets
included; the General's disgust was so great that suddenly he tore off one of
the bonnets and urinated into it.

In many ways Liu Pang was the kind of practical man admired by those
whose downfall he sought. But it was just this lack of education and knowledge that permitted him to adopt a more flexible and pragmatic approach
than his aristocratic predecessors, and which sealed the initial success of his
dynasty. These qualities were also shown by the fact that, as he assumed the
throne, he became increasingly aware of his responsibilities. In retrospect,
we see not only that he was influenced by Confucianism, but also that he
adopted much of the theory into his method of government.

*Previous page : Pottery roof-tile end
with a moulded design of a phoenix, or
red bird, symbol of the south. These
tile ends became popular vehicles for
the expression of traditional, mythological and symbolical ideas*

*Right : Portrait of the founding
Emperor of the Han Dynasty, Kao
Tsu. Drawing from the* San-ts'ai
t'u-hui *(1609 edition)*

漢高祖像

59

漢景帝像

Once Liu Pang had defeated the other principal contender, his one-time commander Hsiang Yü, he established his capital at Ch'ang-an (the modern city of Sian), and founded the Han Dynasty, taking the name of Kao Tsu. The *History of the Former Han Dynasty*, or *Han Shu*, written by Pan Ku in the first century AD, records an illuminating description of him: 'Kao Tsu was a man with a prominent nose and a dragon forehead. He had a beautiful beard on his chin and cheeks. On his left thigh were seventy-two black moles. He was kindly disposed to others, benevolent and liked people. His mind was vast.' Seventy-two moles may seem an excessive number, but they hold all kinds of mystic associations, for this was the number of the days in one year attributed to each of the five elements (earth, metal, water, wood and fire) and the number of ancient sovereigns who had performed the great sacrifices.

The description continues:

He liked wine and women. He frequently went to an old dame Wang and an old lady Wu to buy wine on credit. While he was sleeping off the effects of the wine, the old lady Wu and the old woman Wang frequently saw wonderful sights above him. Every time Kao Tsu came to buy some wine, he would stay and drink, and they would sell several times more and when they saw the wonderful sights, the two shopkeepers at the end of the year would often break up the accounts and forgive the debt.

But it was no easy task that Kao Tsu faced in consolidating this new dynasty. Above all, he faced threats from two main sources. First, the menace of the old Ch'in rulers whose despotic centralised authority he had broken down; second, the external threat of 'barbarians', the Huns of the north and north-west. Termed 'Hsiung-nu' by the Chinese, these tribal steppe peoples, generally of similar Mongoloid stock but Turkish-speaking, were the same that had earlier threatened the Ch'in and led to the construction of the Great Wall. They were developing a basically nomadic society which differed completely from the stable agricultural framework of the Yellow River basin. But they, too, were subject to the vagaries of the elements and occasional drastic food shortages drew them towards the rich agricultural lands of the Middle Kingdom. Their more mobile way of life, based on the horse, meant they could make rapid incursions into Chinese territory, and the more cumbersome chariots of the Chinese, accompanied by foot soldiers, were no match for the fleet cavalry from Mongolia and south Russia. They even managed to ride within sight of the capital in 166 BC.

61

Left: Portrait of Prince Liu Sheng's father, the Emperor Ching. Drawing from the San-ts'ai t'u-hui *(1609 edition)*

To combat the menace of the old Ch'in aristocracy, Kao Tsu was forced to revert in part to the political divisions of earlier times. Thus he gave feoffs to his followers but made a rule that only a member of the Imperial family could be made a king. But he was cautious not to provide any opportunities for these vassal lords and kings to gain significant power. Their territories were considerably smaller than those of the Late Chou feudal rulers, and in addition Kao frequently displaced them. Either they were degraded or given new territories elsewhere in the Empire. The Emperor was quite ruthless in his actions, for even Han Hsin, one of Kao's closest allies and generals in the wars against Hsiang Yü, was degraded and finally executed.

Kao adopted other aspects of the Ch'in system. In addition to the feudal kings he used central government officials to rule a patchwork of minor states throughout the Empire. Thus, although he had on purely practical grounds dismissed the centralised form of government, he had also created a loose form of decentralised power in order to minimise the threat of substantial revolt from within. But the kind of problem facing Kao Tsu is vividly described in the *Han Shu*; a quote from the entry for the year 201 BC reads:

When the Emperor had already appointed to noble positions twenty-odd men of great merits, the rest disputed over their merits for those enfeoffments . . . which had not yet been made. When the Emperor was in the Southern Palace, from one of the connecting terraces between halls, he saw the generals often talking together privately. He asked Chang Liang about this, and Chang replied: 'Your Majesty conquered the world together with these people. Now you are already the Son of Heaven, and those whom you have enfeoffed are all your old friends and those whom you love, while those whom you have punished with death were all enemies you have made in your lifetime, and against whom you held a grudge. Now the army officers are counting up those who have merits and think that the world is insufficient to enfeoff them all, so they fear that for a small fault they might meet with the punishment of death. Hence they meet and plan to rebel.' The Emperor replied: 'What can I do about it?' Chang Liang then said: 'Take the persons whom Your Majesty has always disliked, select out one whom all your courtiers know you dislike most of all, and enfeoff him first in order to show your courtiers that you mean well.' In the third month the Emperor held a feast and enfeoffed Yung Ch'ih. Thereupon he urged his Lieutenant Chancellor to hasten and determine the merits of the officers and make appropriate appointments. When the feast was over, the courtiers were all glad and said: 'Even Yung Ch'ih has been appointed a marquis, we have no cause for anxiety.'

62 This is a typical example of the manœuvrings and intrigue which the rulers

Right : Pottery tomb model of a five-storeyed tower set in a small courtyard with watchtowers at each corner. It is models such as this which provide us with information about Han architecture.

had to accomplish in order to maintain peace at court.

Apart from these enfeoffed kings and nobles, the actual business of government was handled by that most Confucian and characteristically Chinese social phenomenon – the official. The concept of the official or *Chün-tzu* obtaining his distinguished position through fortunate birth had disappeared in the Ch'in, and Kao Tsu continued the tradition of appointment through education and examination. This may already be seen as a concession to Confucianism. The officials were accorded a rank within the hierarchy and certainly never lost the status and dignity now generally accorded them.

The position of the official class is illustrated in the Chinese histories. From these writings a picture of a highly complex civil service emerges; one in which grade and privilege were protected and revered. The structure of government provided for the steady promotion of the official from a junior to senior post, and with their gradual rise through the hierarchy they duly incurred further privileges, benefits and dignity. The official view of the official is described thus in an edict of 144 BC: 'Now the officials are the teachers of the people. It is proper that their carriages and quadriges, their clothes and robes should correspond to their dignity.' The edict then goes on to describe at length precisely how the carriages of officials of each grade should be painted. For example: 'We order that on carriages of important officials ranked at two thousand piculs [a variable weight measure, usually about 133 lb, which represented the annual stipend, in grain, of the officials] both side screens should be painted vermilion; and on those of officials whose positions are ranked from one thousand to six hundred piculs the left screen only should be vermilion.' This same edict goes on to say that any official who 'departs into the hamlets' not garbed according to his rank should be reported to the Lieutenant Chancellor who 'shall beg the throne to order them to be punished'.

One of the major problems facing Kao Tsu was finding enough officials to operate the ever-expanding government machine. In 196 BC, he issued an edict to senior officials of the states and commanderies throughout the kingdom requesting that they should send likely candidates to the capital for examination. The *Han Shu* records:

Now I, by the spiritual power of heaven, and by my capable gentlemen and high officials have subjugated and possess the Empire and made it into one family. I

Right : Pair of jade pendants in the form of dragons with granulation patterns on the surface. Late Chou Dynasty, fourth–third centuries BC

wish it to be enduring so that generation after generation should worship at my ancestral temple. Capable persons have already shared with me in its pacification. Should it be that any capable persons are not to share together with me in its comfort and its benefits? If there are any capable gentlemen or sirs who are willing to follow and be friends with me, I can make them honourable and illustrious. . . .

This was also a useful way for the Emperor to gain widespread loyalties by drawing upon people from all regions to staff his government.

These, in broad terms, were the principles of government instituted by the first Emperor of Han. The system derived substantially from the preceding Ch'in, and was to change very little for the next two thousand years. Its two principal characteristics became permanent features of Chinese society. First, there was the status of the officials, that favoured élite, educated in the Classics, virtuous, worthy and held in the highest regard as the representatives of the Emperor. The officials formed a hierarchy quite distinct from the aristocracy, men like Prince Liu Sheng, who ruled the enfeoffed states and kingdoms, which were the hereditary possessions of privileged lines. In the Late Chou period the *Chün-tzu* had been an inherited position, which no doubt caused the irreconcilably reactionary attitudes adopted by them at that time. But the Han continued in the Ch'in tradition of appointment and promotion through examination.

In spite of Kao Tsu's initial dislike of Confucianism he instituted a system of government through professional scholars of which Confucius himself would have heartily approved. As the Han government and institutions became established an official class developed and with it, certain benefits accrued to official families. For example, opportunities arose for the advancement of their sons into an official government position which would not be so easily available to the commoner.

As the general wealth of the Han Empire increased so there emerged a social class new to China, the merchants, traders and businessmen. However they were by no means accorded the status and dignity of the scholar-official – a sure sign of the impact of the Confucian ideal. The position of the merchant in Early Han society is made clear in an Imperial edict of 199 BC, during the reign of Kao Tsu. It reads: 'Merchants are not to be permitted to wear brocade, embroidery, flowered silk, crêpe linen, sackcloth or wool, carry weapons, or ride a quadrige or a horse.'

65

Top left : Twin-cupped vessel, made of gilt bronze inlaid with jade, and decorated with a phoenix, traditionally the symbol of the empress in China. A jade ring is suspended from the beak of the phoenix. From the tomb of the

Princess Tou Wan

Bottom left : Two of a set of bronze leopards with partial gilding. From the tomb of Princess Tou Wan

The second principal consequence of Kao Tsu's system was the degree of autonomy permitted the enfeoffed states. However, we have seen how he combatted too much independence by breaking down the large Chou states into smaller units and by appointing loyal followers as their rulers. In this respect, again, his more pragmatic approach allowed him to develop new ideas of government and to abandon concepts of ancient hierarchy. One important aspect was, however, constant. That was the derivation of all power from the Emperor himself. From him and his closest advisers authority was transmitted through the officials of the central government in the capital city to the local administrative organs.

With Kao Tsu's tough, uncompromising and yet realistic rule the foundations of the Han were laid. It was an auspicious beginning, although the best was yet to come. The reign of the Emperor Wu Ti from 141 to 87 BC is generally and justifiably considered as the apogee of Han power. He ascended the throne at the tender age of fifteen and a half, and yet seems to have been in no way overawed by his predicament. He was a man of tremendous energy and adopted an increasingly autocratic position.

Kao Tsu had established an elaborate machinery for the management of the Han Empire, in which the officials played a vital part. His immediate successors developed and refined this system – until Wu Ti. The unwritten law of China located the Emperor at the summit of the political and social structure, but left the running of the country to his highly placed bureaucrats. Wu Ti overthrew this traditional hierarchy and increasingly took on the duties of government, acting more as a prime minister than as a head of state or monarch. His actions set a precedent, for subsequent governments tended to alternate between eras of personal administration by dynamic emperors and eras of government by the bureaucrats. Traditionally the Emperor was beyond reproach and could do no wrong. Periods of Imperial rule, such as Wu Ti's, tended therefore to end in disaster because no check, criticism or reformation of his decisions and actions could be made. This forms a contrast to the less decisive, but generally more flexible and stable, rule under the bureaucrats.

Like all autocrats, Wu Ti gathered round him a close circle of friends and advisers to whom he gave privileges, often without considering the political implications of his actions. For example, he appointed the relatives of his

66

Right : Rubbing taken from a brick relief showing the entrance to a Han palace, with watchtowers flanking the doorway. Above is the phoenix, or red bird, symbol of the south. From a tomb near Ch'eng-tu in Szechwan

favourite women to important positions as officials, without regard to their ability or judgement. Thus intrigues and manipulations at Court became rife. A further complication was provided by the intervention of the Empress Dowager, Wu Ti's mother. The role of the Empress Dowager in Chinese history has always been notorious, culminating in the extraordinary antics and prejudices of the last, the Empress Dowager Tzu Hsi, who died at the beginning of this century.

Wu Ti, almost inevitably in the social context of China, trusted his mother and permitted considerable freedom in the Court and in government circles.

By the Confucian virtue of filial piety he was also required to obey her, and thus the circle of intrigue and misplaced power was constructed. The adverse influence of the female element behind the throne, generally in the form of the Empress since she was the one who would command obedience, arose out of the fact that these Court ladies were virtually imprisoned in the Imperial palaces and grounds. Their contact with, knowledge and under-standing of the outside world, the practical problems of the government and the people, were negligible, and yet they were able to wield immense power. History has shown them to be among the most reactionary and destructive elements in Chinese history.

Right from the outset of his reign this was a major problem which the young Wu Ti had to face. Almost his first action as Emperor was to honour the Empress Dowager with the title 'Grand Empress Dowager'. Within three months of his enthronement he had enfeoffed both the younger brothers of the Empress Dowager, and given them the title of 'marquis'. In spite of these difficulties and the whole aura of intrigue and suspicion among his relatives and the Imperial family at Court, Wu Ti was sufficiently forthright and strong to remain very much in control. The real effects of what was going on behind the scenes were not to be felt until after his death, when potentially disruptive elements felt at liberty to take advantage of their position.

Literally translated, the title Wu Ti means 'Military Emperor'. It was a fitting description for Wu Ti because his military endeavours and expansion of the Empire were his greatest achievements. These military exploits were carried out on two broad fronts; in the northern and north-western frontier lands and in the south. The campaigns in the north were, in a sense, defen-sively inspired, while those in the south were in the interests of expansion and to a lesser extent trade.

In the north it was the familiar enemy with whom Wu Ti had to contend, the Hunnish Hsiung-nu. As a result of these wars, China came to control huge tracts of barren land in Central Asia: parts of Mongolia, southern Russia, the endless wastes of the Gobi Desert, and across the Tarim Basin to Ferghana and Sodgiana, and the northern borders of present-day Afghanistan. Wu Ti also expanded Han territories in the north-west when he occupied most of Manchuria and northern Korea, then a semi-Chinese state called Chosōn, in an attempt to outflank the Hsiung-nu.

68   In order to combat the Hsiung-nu, the Emperor had to mount massive

Right : A modern view of a typical Chinese palace garden. This example, dating from the nineteenth century, is in Shanghai. The ornamental lake is fundamental to the landscaped garden in China.

70

*Two details of a pottery tomb model of
a watchtower, showing the lively
naturalism that characterised much
Han tomb art. The circular motifs on
the eaves are pottery roof-tile ends.
Western Han Dynasty*

expeditions which must have put the Imperial coffers under considerable strain. The Chinese histories seldom describe the battles fought by these massive armies, or indeed tell much about the soldiers' apparel, appearance or weaponry. However, occasional paintings or sculptured reliefs illustrate, perhaps none too accurately, these remote and bloody events. The charm and naïvety of these Han pictures belie the nature of the events they depict. The use of the cavalry was of course inherited from the horse-riding Huns, who were no doubt much more proficient than their Chinese foes. Also, virtually all the Hun soldiers were mounted whereas, as we have seen from the entries in the *Han Shu*, the Chinese troops were usually approximately one-third cavalry to two-thirds foot soldiers. This at least is reflected in many of the pictorial representations, where we see two sets of cavalry confronting one another, the Chinese forces backed up with rows of kneeling crossbow-men. As we have already seen in connection with the Great Wall, the Chinese were more accustomed to stationary warfare; their principal aim was defensive, especially in these northern and north-western border lands.

Although we speak of the triumph of Confucianism in the Han, it was by no means an instantaneous procedure. The founder, Kao Tsu, was as we have seen the complete autocrat, while his feelings about the Confucian scholar were made abundantly clear on one occasion. Wu Ti was hardly more liberal in his control. But both recognised the need for educated men in government and so gradually there arose a certain class of scholar whose services provided the foundations of government. This is proven in an edict issued by Wu Ti in the summer of 124 BC which runs:

Truly it is said that one should lead the people by the rules of proper conduct and influence them by music. But now the rules of proper conduct have fallen into ruin and the standards of music have crumbled. We are very much saddened by this. Thus we have diligently sought to obtain the gentlemen of great renown throughout the Empire and have had them all recommended to the various courts. Let it be ordered that the officials for the rites should encourage study, discourse on rights and duties, broaden scholarship, present documents to the court, and promote the rules of proper conduct, in order that they may lead the world. Let the Grand Master of Ceremonies discuss the giving of disciples to the erudite, for the promoting of cultural influence in the districts and villages in order to encourage those who are capable and able. The Lieutenant Chancellor, Kung-sun

72

Right: A rubbing from a Han Dynasty stone relief, showing an official in his carriage being pulled by four slaves, and another attendant at the rear

Hung, begged the throne that for the erudite there should be established a definite number of disciples. And so scholars increased greatly in number.

In this announcement, Wu Ti openly acknowledges that those Confucian qualities of which his predecessor, Kao Tsu, once so disapproved were just the ones required to maintain a stable government. The last section of the edict is perhaps the most significant, since it announces the foundation of a kind of Imperial institution for the training of officials, at the instigation of Kung-sun Hung. At first there were just fifty students, destined for government service, but by the time of the Later Han Dynasty (first and second centuries AD), the number had grown to a staggering thirty thousand. With all these officials trained in the Confucian virtues, the Confucian standards and way of life, and educated in the ancient Classics, it was natural that Confucianism gradually became the official philosophy of the state.

It is a typical ambiguity of China that a reign which, with all justification, has gone down in history as one of great military exploits and achievements should also witness the assimilation of a philosophy of government and society which was founded on study, education, the Classics of ancient

literature and culture. Wu Ti was without doubt closer to the Legalist ideal when he first ascended the throne but made it more palatable to the people and more lasting and flexible as a form of government by the gradual incorporation of Confucianism.

All the same, Wu Ti was a tough and uncompromising person to those whom he trusted and had placed in high positions, an attitude illustrated by his reaction to an unsuccessful campaign against the Huns in 129 BC:

. . . their colonels [of the Generals of Tai and Yen-men commanderies] moreover turned their backs upon their duty and acted senselessly in deserting the army and fleeing . . . in accordance with the laws governing the use of troops, failure in being diligent or in instructing the troops is the fault of a general or leader and when instructions have been given, not to be able to use all his power in executing these orders is the crime of an officer or soldier. These generals have already been given into the charge of the Commandant of Justice, who is to apply the law and execute them. But if this law is also applied to the soldiers so that both generals and troops are punished then this would not be the way of a benevolent or sage person. We pity the crowd of common soldiers when they have sunk into this disastrous situation and wish to eradicate their disgrace, change their conduct and once more act according to their rightful duty, but they have no way of doing so . . . let the soldiers of Tai and Yen-men be pardoned.

We see here a distinct sympathy with the common man, in complete contrast to the remote unconcerned attitudes of the ancient emperors. It is highlighted again by an edict of 140 BC, right at the beginning of Wu Ti's reign, which states: 'The guards for transport and post services and for escorting people to and from the capital number twenty thousand men. Let them be reduced by ten thousand men, and the Imperial pastures and their horses to be abolished in order that these lands may be used by the poor people.'

The reign of Wu Ti was indeed a great one; the apogee of Han power. His intended achievement was the extension and consolidation of the Empire. But in retrospect his most important contribution was perhaps the one which he made somewhat reluctantly: the assimilation of Confucian ideals into the governmental system which became the hall-mark of later China. The *Han Shu* eloquently sums up his reign:

The Han Dynasty inherited the evils of the many kings; the eminent founder [Kao Tsu] established order out of confusion and made things right. The attentions of the Emperors Wen and Ching were directed towards the concerns of the common people, but in matters of investigating ancient practices and of respecting literature they still had many defects. When Emperor Wu first came to the throne he abolished and dismissed the study of many non-Confucian schools of philosophy in a surprising way, and thus made known and rendered illustrious the six Confucian classics. Thereupon he had all the officials within the four seas 'search for intelligent persons who could accord with the times and recommend those who were talented and excellent'; he gave them the opportunity to distinguish themselves. He founded the Imperial University, renewed certain sacrifices, corrected the new year and fixed the calculation of the calendar, harmonised musical notes and tunes, composed songs and music, established the sacrifices of *feng* and *shan*, and worshipped the various divinities. His commands and edicts, his writings and literary compositions are splendid and may be transmitted for posterity so that his descendants may follow his grand achievements and possess the fame of the great dynasties.

If Emperor Wu, with his superior ability and his great plans had not departed from the modesty and economy of the Emperors Wen and Ching, and if by means of these principles he had helped the common people, in what respects could any of those heroes who are praised in the Book of Odes or the Book of History have surpassed him?

One of the inevitable consequences of Wu Ti's successful Imperial expansion was a general rise in the wealth of the state. At the same time there came an increase in the population, and it was this that was to prove his stumbling-block. As the population grew, each peasant family had less land to cultivate and could, therefore, less and less afford the taxes demanded by the central government. In addition, a large number of peasants were farming on the tax-free estates of the aristocracy. Prince Liu Sheng himself paid no taxes on his territories and had peasant farmers working the land. Thus state revenues were declining by the end of Wu Ti's reign, but not of course his expenditure on military expeditions and Imperial households.

Another consequence of Wu Ti's impact was that his successors tried to emulate him. These were competent but unexceptional men, who merely continued to build on the foundations laid by their illustrious predecessor. Emperor Hsiao-Ai (reigned 7–1 BC) was, however, a different proposition, for he tried to imitate the 'strong' government of Wu but succeeded only in becoming a tool of the Imperial family. This was the beginning of the decline of the Former Han Dynasty, when the Court became rife with intrigue and opportunism. The position concerning relatives of the Imperial family had changed somewhat since the reign of Emperor Wu. With the increasing accept- 75

ance of the Confucian philosophy into government came the increasing power and influence of the relatives of the Emperor. Those on the paternal side were all potential rivals for the throne, and thus Prince Liu Sheng might at some time, had he been perhaps more concerned with his duties and politically ambitious, have found himself in a position to acquire the 'Mandate of Heaven'.

The principal contenders for power at the Court were the families of Chao and Wang. The latter clan first married into the Imperial house in the reign of the Emperor Yüan (49–33 BC) and went from strength to strength, primarily through the influence of the Grand Empress Dowager Wang, mother of the Emperor Ch'eng (33–7 BC). Once again the figure of an Empress Dowager looms forbiddingly on the horizon. The Chao clan owed its position to the Emperor Ch'eng's second wife, Chao Fei-yen. She became the adopted mother of Emperor Hsiao-Ai and consequently she was appointed Empress Dowager. However the Chao clan were eliminated as contenders when a scandal concerning Chao Fei-yen's younger sister and the Emperor Ch'eng was discovered. The story of these bizarre events typifies the goings-on at the Imperial Court.

After Chao Fei-yen's elevation to Empress, the Emperor lost interest in her and became infatuated with her younger sister. She was made a 'Brilliant Companion' (the highest rank among Imperial concubines) and installed in the Sun Bright Residence, the most prominent of the eight halls of the Imperial Harem. Here she lived in the most opulent surroundings – the hall painted with gold and bedecked with jewels. The Emperor promised to be faithful to her, but Ch'eng was something of a philanderer and his attentions wandered to a slave girl, Ts'ao Kung, who in 12 BC announced that she was pregnant by the Emperor. Since neither of the Chao sisters had borne any children, this girl and her child constituted a considerable threat to their position, for if the child became the Heir Apparent, its mother would be made Empress and the Chao sisters would lose their position and influence.

Soon after, a eunuch came to the assistant at the harem prison with an edict stating that the slave girl Ts'ao Kung, her child and her six slaves be taken to the palace prison, and that it should never be asked what sex the child was or who the father was. Within days another edict arrived from the Emperor asking if the child was dead. This was followed by yet another message, this time jointly from the Emperor and the Brilliant Companion expressing anger that the assistant had not yet killed mother and child. By the time the child was seven or eight days old, another eunuch was given

Right : Pottery tomb model of a palanquin bearer, probably from the tomb of the official or noble he had once served. Eastern Han Dynasty

Far right : Small pottery tomb model of a kneeling servant : the type of figure which would have been buried with the dead master to attend to his needs in the after-life

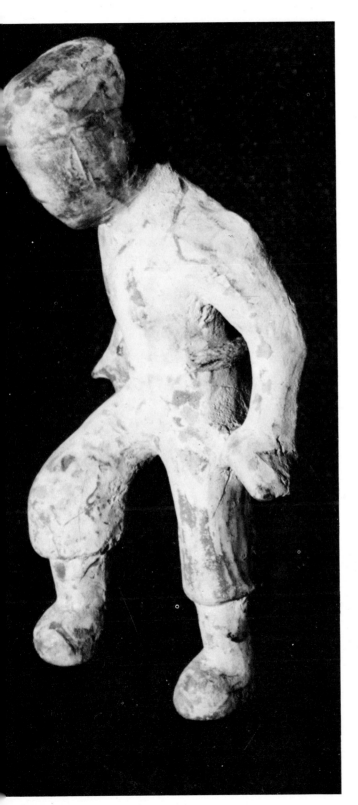

charge and instructed to select a wet-nurse for the baby and, of course, to keep the utmost secrecy about the whole affair. This same eunuch was then given a sealed box with orders that the contents must be given to the mother. Inside were drugs and a note from the Emperor saying: 'I am commanding you, Wei-ning [Ts'ao Kung's title] to try hard to drink this medicine. You cannot enter our presence, which you yourself know.'

The harsh sequel to these events was that Ts'ao Kung drank the poison and died, the six slaves were made to strangle themselves and the baby taken by a eunuch and never seen again. This was not the only case of infanticide in the Imperial Court during Ch'eng's reign. These events, when they were finally known, disgraced the name of Chao and the family fell from contention in the tussles during Hsiao-Ai's reign, leaving the way open for the Wang family to claim ascendancy.

To the people of China these affairs of their Imperial family meant little, and it is hardly likely that they knew much about them. But to the officials at the Court and the contending families it was all very relevant, and strikingly clear that the very core of the Han line was corrupt and degraded. To Wang Mang, Chief Minister under Emperor Ai, it was a cue, with the help of the Empress Dowager, to take the initiative. Under the cloak of restoring Confucian qualities and ideals to the throne, Wang gradually assumed control. He does not sound an attractive proposition; contemporary records describe him as 'a man who had a large mouth and a receding chin, bulging eyes with brilliant pupils, and a loud voice which was hoarse . . . he was seven feet five inches tall, loved thick-soled shoes and tall bonnets . . . he stuck out his chest and made himself look tall so that he could look down on those around him . . .'. Wang's moment came when the Emperor P'ing died in February 6 AD. An edict, dated 3 February in that year, runs: 'At that time, the line of descent from Emperor Yüan had been ended, but of the great-grandsons of Emperor Hsüan there were living; five kings and forty-eight marquises. Wang Mang hated it that they were adults and so advised: "A cousin is not permitted to be the successor." So he selected the very youngest of among Emperor Hsüan's great-great-grandsons, Liu Ying. He was in the second year of age.'

It was at this stage that Wang Mang brought into play the supernatural beliefs that had become assimilated into Confucianism. It is recorded that while a well was being dug in a Wu-kung prefecture a white stone was secured, on which was written: 'An instruction to the Duke Giving Tranquility to the Han Dynasty, Wang Mang, that he should become Emperor.' The next move was for the Empress Dowager, she of the Wang clan, to appoint Wang Mang as Regent. This was followed by a series of edicts proclaiming his services to the Han Dynasty in the past which culminated in a memorial issued by various courtiers saying:

The sage virtue of the Grand Empress Dowager is brilliant. You have seen deeply

78

into the intentions of Heaven and have issued an Imperial order that the Duke Giving Tranquility to the Han Dynasty should act as Regent. Your subjects have heard that when King Ch'eng of the Chou Dynasty was a minor and the practices of the Chou Dynasty had not yet been completed, so that King Ch'eng was unable to perform his duties to Heaven and Earth and to renew the illustrious services performed by the Kings Wen and Wu, the Duke of Chou temporarily acted as Regent and the practices of the Chou Dynasty were therefore completed and its kingly house was at peace. If he had not acted as Regent, then it is to be feared that the Chou would have lost the Mandate of Heaven.

This illustrates how the supporters of Wang Mang cleverly found an historical precedent for their champion to receive the 'Mandate of Heaven', supposedly in the cause of maintaining the Han line. In July of that same year, 6 AD, Wang continued in this capacity, gradually assuming more and more the aura of the Son of Heaven, supported of course by auspicious portents and memorials praising his great wisdom and ability, until early in the year 9 AD he went to the Temple of Emperor Kao, bowed, and received the metal casket and the resignation of the Han Dynasty which 'the gods had commanded'. This marks the end of the first Han period, known as the Former Han Dynasty.

Thus Wang's long and tortuous path to the throne was finally achieved. Immediately he threw himself into a series of far-reaching reforms aimed principally at putting the Imperial coffers healthily into the black. Apart from fiscal reforms and the introduction of coins of differing denominations – which incidentally allowed him to amass a vast personal fortune of gold (some five million ounces) – his major achievement was to 'nationalise' land. He did this to combat the enormous tax-free estates of the nobility; parcelling them out among the tax-paying peasants and thereby gaining revenue. In so doing he incurred the intense displeasure of the dispossessed landlords, to such an extent that within three years he was forced to rescind the measure.

In the second year of his reign, 10 AD, Wang Mang introduced further revenue-raising schemes: 'the ordinances for the six monopolies'. These commanded that the Imperial government should (1) dispense liquors; (2) sell salt; (3) sell iron implements; (4) cast cash; (5) tax all mineral workings; and (6) 'that the officers in charge of the market-places should collect things when they were cheap and sell them when expensive, and lend on credit to the common people'. Such an overall intrusion into the normal workings of society, especially in so vast an empire, was bound to fail, and Wang faced minor uprisings against his inflexible rule as soon as these laws were introduced. Far from being the Confucianist he proclaimed, he was in fact more in the Legalist mould.

Of these internal dissenters, by far the most formidable was a group known as the 'Red Eyebrows' (deriving their name from the habit of painting their eyebrows) who Wang Mang considered, like all other dissidents, as

79

nothing more than bandits. But the Red Eyebrows represented something far more significant than a band of roaming thugs. They originated in Shantung province in 18 AD, when the *Han Shu* records: 'In this year, Li Tzu-tu, Fan Ch'ung and others of the Red Eyebrows gathered together because of the famine and arose in Lang-yeh commandery. They moved about and robbed. Their bands all numbered in the ten thousands. Wang Mang sent commissioners to mobilise the troops of the commanderies and kingdoms to attack them, but these troops were unable to conquer the robber bands.'

The Red Eyebrows were, of course, brigands, but inspired not by personal greed but by the ever-worsening circumstances of the peasantry. It was a popular uprising, and these bands of near-desperadoes virtually laid waste vast areas of land, but they had no administrative ability and were therefore unable to consolidate their achievements. In military matters they went from strength to strength, and in 22 AD, a band of 'several ten thousand men were in Liang commandery . . . and the Imperial troops were defeated and fled'. This was an omen for Wang Mang, and an inspiration for the Red Eyebrows and others following in their wake. It was also a propitious moment for the surviving, but now dispossessed, members of the Han line, the Liu family. They recognised that by supporting the rebel bands a way could be paved for their return to power. Wang continued to ridicule the Red Eyebrows in desperate attempts to reassure both himself and his Court: 'These people . . . are merely a crowd of thieves produced by hunger and cold, like dogs and sheep that have gathered together . . . who do not know how to formulate such institutions.'

By this time, 23 AD, the Imperial troops were demoralised, fatigued and disillusioned with the continual and generally unsuccessful battles against the rebel peasants. By the autumn of the same year the troubles had reached breaking-point and even the Court had lost all faith. 'Outside the Court, Wang Mang's armies had been routed and inside the Court his greatest ministers had rebelled, so that none of those about him could be trusted . . .'. Early in October, rebel troops entered the capital city of Ch'ang-an and within two days Wang Mang was killed on top of the 'Tower Bathed by Water' in the palace enclave.

The end of Wang Mang's short rule precipitated a military free-for-all
80   from which Liu Hsiu, a descendant of the Han rulers and prosperous land-

Right : Gilt-bronze wine vessel, hu, *inlaid with turquoise. From the tomb of Prince Liu Sheng*

owner in Honan province, finally emerged as victor. He established the capital at nearby Loyang, reigned for over thirty years (25–57 AD) and established a pattern of dynastic revival that was not only admired by Chinese historians but became a prototype for later restorations. He adopted the title 'Kuang Wu Ti', meaning 'Bright Military Emperor', and showed the type of positive forceful rule which characterised founding reigns. He suppressed the Red Eyebrows and other rebellious groups and re-created the strong centralised government of Kao Tsu and Wu Ti. Above all he restored the Han Dynasty, now known as the 'Later Han'.

Kuang Wu was succeeded by the Emperor Ming (57–75 AD) who carried on the vigorous reconstruction and expansion of his predecessor. As with the Former Han Dynasty, the years of consolidation and reconstruction were followed by years of development and expansion. The glorious years of Wu Ti's reign can be paralleled by those of the Emperor Ming. Under the latter the Han repossessed vast tracts of land in Central Asia, a task made easier by the split of the Hsiung-nu into northern and southern empires.

Outstanding amongst the Chinese military men of the day was Pan Ch'ao, whose brother Pan Ku was the author of the *History of the Former Han Dynasty* (*Han Shu*). It was principally due to his efforts that the Chinese Empire stretched across Central Asia to the shores of the Caspian Sea, with only Parthia separating it from the Roman Empire. Pan was an unrelenting warrior who never seemed to accept defeat; even when ordered by an increasingly timorous Imperial government to evacuate the Tarim Basin he merely made a token gesture of withdrawal, then returned, established himself in Kashgar again and promptly beheaded all those who in the interval had shown disloyalty.

Above all Pan showed how he knew his enemy. In 87 AD, the King of Kashgar rose in revolt, but feigned submission and requested an audience with the Chinese general to discuss terms. He arrived with a sizeable cavalry contingent reckoning to make a surprise attack. Pan realised this, pretended to be taken in by the ploy, and feasted, wined and entertained the King. Then suddenly he seized the King and beheaded him and the Chinese troops he had at the ready dropped their disguise and massacred the opposition. There was clearly no stopping a man of such determination and guile, and the Chinese Empire continued to grow. His influence and inspiration moved   81

Top left : Bronze ritual water vessel,
p'an, with climbing tigers. Warring
States period, circa fifth century BC
Far left : Bronze ritual food vessel,
kuei. Early Chou Dynasty, tenth
century BC

Left : Bronze cowrie-container
excavated at Chin-ning in Yunnan
province. The lid is ornamented with
water buffaloes and a horse and rider.
Western Han Dynasty

the Chinese generals in the north to quell the Huns and take Mongolia.

Pan Ch'ao retired in 102 AD, and returned to the capital, Loyang, bedecked with every kind of honour, but a mere shadow of his former self. He died within a few months. His years of campaigning had been amongst the most ambitious enterprises of the whole Han Dynasty, and extended the sphere of Chinese influence further than ever before. After his death history once more repeated itself. His followers were pale reflections, like the Emperors who succeeded Kuang Wu and Ming, and we enter into the now familiar pattern of weak emperors, Court intrigue and popular uprisings.

As was now customary, the troubles began with those closest to the throne, the relatives of the Emperor. The Empresses once adopted by the Son of Heaven found endless opportunities for extending their wealth and power, and sought to consolidate it by bringing their own relatives into the game. To combat this ever-growing 'family' of seekers of power and wealth, the Emperors turned to the Court eunuchs. When, in 159 AD, the high Court eunuchs finally extinguished a powerful clan, the Liang, the five leading eunuchs were enfeoffed with enormous holdings of lands. Now, like the families they had helped to wipe out, they saw potential wealth and power within their grasp.

The inevitable consequence was conflict between the powerful eunuchs and the remnants of the aristocratic landowning families. As in the past, the internecine warfare that followed resulted in massive loss of life and the total breakdown of both government and bureaucracy. The great purges carried out by the eunuchs between 170 and 180 AD affected the whole country, and no section of society, from Imperial family to lowly peasant, was safe.

Popular uprisings against the rampant eunuchs developed in all parts of the Empire but none was so successful as the itinerant magician, Chang Chüeh. The now dispirited and dispossessed peasantry were ready to follow anybody who promised a brighter future, and Chang had a persuasive ability inspired by his mysterious powers of alchemy. Magical beliefs with strong Taoist tendencies developed swiftly during these years of unrest, for there seemed to the populace less and less reason to have any faith in the old Imperial tradition and in Confucian bureaucracy. Whether Chang Chüeh had any medical ability is quite another matter, but he certainly had remarkable success with his cure, consisting of drinking pure water over which a formula had already been pronounced. With the massive support of the peasants in the central and eastern provinces, Chang took up the cudgels against both the tyrannical administration and the highly unpopular eunuchs.

Chang and his bands of followers wore a distinguishing head-dress from which they derived their name – the 'Yellow Turbans'. They swept through the countryside with a remorseless dedication to destruction, and they were

82

Above : An official in his canopied carriage. Bronze tomb model from an Eastern Han tomb at Leitai in Kansu province

to prove the principal cause of the downfall of the house of Liu and the Later Han Dynasty. Although Chang himself was killed in 184 AD, the Yellow Turbans lived on as a great popular revolution and they were the inspiration for many of the later secret revolutionary societies in China. Some of these claimed to have inherited the secret magical instructions of Chang, the formula for the secret elixir which he gave his followers just before they entered battle, thus promising their immortality. Even the Boxers in their 1900 rebellion held to this same magic.

In the westerly province of Szechwan another Taoist-inspired rebellious group, known as the 'Five Pecks of Rice' band, caused further disruption to an already disintegrating Empire. Their strange name was derived from the dues which followers paid to their cult leaders. They operated in much the same way as the Yellow Turbans, rampaging through the countryside causing death and destruction, motivated by magical Taoist ideas and inspired by ideals of peasant revolt against a hopelessly corrupt government.

And so the Later Han Dynasty came to a rather messy end. An end which bears a striking resemblance to those of the Chou and Former Han periods. As the power of the central government diminished, so did their ability to raise and maintain an army, and it fell to the rich landlords to provide their own defence. Once again it was these private professional armies that became dominant, finally crushing the eunuchs and the massive popular uprisings. Gradually power became divided among the three leading generals: Ts'ao Ts'ao, the son of an adopted son of a eunuch in the north; Sun Ch'üan in the south-east, and in the west Prince Liu Sheng's family found a continuing champion in Liu Pei, who controlled the province of Szechwan where the Five Pecks of Rice band had once held sway.

Although effective control of the Han Empire was in the hands of these three, the Han Dynasty still nominally existed. It was not until 220 AD, when Ts'ao Ts'ao died and his son Ts'ao Pei followed, that the Han finally came to an end. Ts'ao Pei usurped the throne and established the Wei Dynasty; although, of course, he ruled only in the north. Sun Ch'üan followed suit in the south-east and established the Wu Dynasty, and Liu Pei of the Han Imperial family established the Shu Han in Szechwan and the west. For the next half century China remained divided into these three independent kingdoms, and was not to find real unity until the establishment of the Sui Dynasty in 581, nearly four centuries later.

5 THE COURT OF THE SON OF HEAVEN

DOMINATING THE LIFE AT THE COURT OF THE HAN DYNASTY WAS the spectre of a man, seldom seen but ever present, the Son of Heaven, the Emperor. He stood at the apex of the pyramid of Chinese society. Beneath him were the officials and then the largest unit of all, the common people. These broad distinctions in Chinese society were constant throughout her Imperial history and the foundation of the strictly maintained hierarchy.

First, let us look at the life of the Emperor, in particular Liu Sheng's father, the Emperor Ching, who reigned from 157 to 140 BC. Like all Emperors he was, theoretically at least, the sole source of authority – the Son of Heaven and intermediary between heaven and earth. As we know, Ching's ancestor and founder of the Dynasty, Liu Pang, was a man of humble origins. Having emerged as champion, he acceded to the 'people's wish' and accepted the 'Mandate of Heaven'. Suddenly, therefore, he was transformed from mere man to a figure of almost divine authority and power. Although Liu finally defeated the Ch'in at the end of the year 207 BC, it was not until the beginning of 202 BC that he officially assumed the title of Emperor. Then his grateful vassal kings stated:

You, great King, arose from small beginnings; you destroyed the seditious dynasty of Ch'in; Your Majesty stirs everything within the seas, moreover, starting from a secluded and mean region, from Han-chung, you acted out your majesty and virtue, executing the unrighteous, setting up the meritorious, tranquilising and establishing the Empire. Meritorious officials all received territories and the income of towns; you did not appropriate them for yourself. Your virtue, great King, has been bestowed the breadth and width of the four seas. We, vassal kings are inadequate to express your achievement. For you to take the position of Emperor would be most appropriate. We hope that, you, great King, will favour the world and do so.

Liu acceded as expected to this rather ingratiating but typically laudatory expression of his favoured subjects. The Grand Commandant and others of the highest aristocracy were instructed to choose a 'favourable day', and selected the *chia-wu* day, 28 February 202 BC. Before accepting, Liu declined for the customary three times. From the moment he was enthroned, a cocoon was constructed around the Emperor to distinguish him from the other members of society, to enhance his dignity and authority and above all to provide a cloak of awe and mystery. He was removed from the life of the commonplace which, to Liu Pang particularly, had once been so familiar.

86

Previous page : Pottery tomb figure of a lady of the Court, with ornate triple-pointed headgear. Eastern Han Dynasty

Right : Impressed pottery brick depicting officials dining ; below is a landscape frieze. Eastern Han Dynasty

Now housed in the inner sanctum of the Palace, the Emperor was far removed from the prying eyes of the curious, from the perhaps unpleasant sight of a suffering peasantry, and protected by endless guards and servants from persistent and unwelcome petitioners.

The list of attendants to the Emperor and the Imperial household reflects the grandeur of their living style and compares with that of ancient Greece and Rome. During the reign of the second Emperor, Hui, an edict announced the upgrading 'one step' of the commoners in the household and mentions

the following: Gentlemen of the Household, Gentlemen outside the Household, Gentlemen of the Palace, Eunuchs, Masters of the Food, Palace Messengers, Guards, Spear Bearers, Men of War, Grooms, Chariot Drivers, Chariot Companions and Accessory Officials

We have already had occasion to speak of the eunuchs and the power and influence they managed to acquire. In the Palace their function was to attend to much of the day-to-day administration and running of the household, but their real source of influence stemmed from their duties in the women's apartments. It was here that they managed to accumulate information and to learn of the secrets and favouritisms between the Emperor and his concubines. In addition, the highly confidential and trustworthy position of Palace Secretary was generally held by a eunuch. In this capacity the eunuch attended the Emperor when he was at leisure in the women's quarters. Their slightly invidious role in Court rivalries has possibly been overplayed by the historians, but it cannot be denied that in the recorded upsets and scandals in the Palace the eunuchs were invariably involved and generally emerged unscathed and better off.

Because of their much-favoured position the eunuchs were themselves the inspiration of jealousies and controversies, especially those who managed to become close confidants of the Emperor. One such was Chao T'an who, it is recorded, had gained great favour with the Emperor Wen and his successor, the Emperor Ching, due to his knowledge of numerology. For some reason he took a deep dislike to the high official and adviser to the Emperor, Yüan Ang, who was a man of the highest principles and commanded great respect. Perhaps Chao saw the virtuous and dedicated Yüan as a threat to his position.

Yüan Chung, the son of Yüan Ang's older brother, and a horseman in the Emperor's retinue, advised his uncle to have 'an open conflict with Chao T'an and shame him before the court, so that the Emperor will pay no more attention to his slander.' So one day, when the Emperor left the Palace, Yüan Ang prostrated himself before the carriage and said: 'I have always been told that only the most distinguished men of the Empire are privileged to ride with the Son of Heaven in his six-foot carriage of state. Now although the Han may be lacking in worthy men I cannot imagine why Your Majesty would deign to ride in the same carriage with a man who is no more than a remnant of the knife and saw [this is a term of contempt for eunuchs].' The Emperor laughed and ordered a weeping Chao T'an out of the carriage.

88

Right : Pair of small jade figures of Court ladies wearing long flowing robes, said to have come from Sian-fu in Shensi province. Eastern Han Dynasty

Although only an insignificant event, it does illustrate the power of the eunuchs to upset and provoke even the most respected and diffident of the upper echelons of the hierarchy.

The Imperial Palaces of the Former (or Western) Han Dynasty in the capital city of Ch'ang-an (the modern city of Sian, capital of Shensi province) were built with little regard for expense. And, of course, there were ancillary palaces for special occasions or recreations, such as the Imperial hunting-palaces or those erected for the Empress Dowager or a favoured concubine. The Palace of Sweet Springs was typical of these; generally used for Imperial hunting parties, it was also used by the great Emperor Wu for convalescing. It was probably much like those at Ch'ang-an, comprising a number of audience halls each with a throne, where the Emperor would receive visitors or courtiers, these connected by terraced passages passing through ornate and secluded gardens and enclosed courtyards. The principal buildings would certainly have been built of stone or brick with glazed tile roofs. The ends of the tiles at the eaves were finished with decorative pottery medallions carrying designs conveying messages of good augury, often a phoenix or dragon, both beasts of good fortune in China, or short invocations of eternal life and prosperity. The whole Imperial enclosure would have been surrounded by a wall of stamped earth or bricks, like the city wall itself, and interspersed with watchtowers. These may have been just two storeys or perhaps three or four and were generally made of wood with thatched roofs. Two such towers would have flanked the imposing gateway to the Palace.

In Ch'ang-an itself, in addition to the Emperor and his immediate retinue, there was an immense permanent staff of servants, concubines, Imperial relatives, grooms and miscellaneous attendants to be housed. Most of the buildings for the staff were on much less grand a scale, not brick or stone but clay and wattle with thatch roofing. But even these more lowly buildings were brightly painted, particularly red in the Han Dynasty, so that the over-all picture of the Imperial Palace and its surrounding buildings would be bright and colourful to contrast with the more sombre browns and greys of the artisan dwellings beyond the compound. Inside the audience halls and private chambers the rich silk hangings, woven, embroidered or painted, the bronze vessels, some of which were inlaid with gold, silver, malachite or turquoise, and the brightly coloured lacquers would have 89 added depth to the distinguishing richness of the Emperor's home.

The Forbidden City in Peking as it stands today, with a series of impressive audience halls flanked by arrays of ancillary buildings, the whole surrounded by a wall and a moat, adopts the same principle as its Han predecessor of some seventeen centuries earlier. Beyond the west wall of the city of Ch'ang-an were situated the Imperial Pleasure Gardens stocked with botanical rarities and beauties from all parts of the Empire, and animals quite unfamiliar to that part of China. The inventive and imaginative landscaping of ornamental gardens has long been an achievement of the Chinese and it is sure that those of the Han emperors at Ch'ang-an were no exception. Ornamental lakes for their pleasure were dotted among the rock gardens and parklands, with ornate towers and secluded pavilions.

The daily routine of Emperor Ching, like others of the Han Dynasty, is not recorded in any detail. However, the annals record the constant comings and goings of officials, courtiers and vassal kings. One may surmise that audiences with these and attendances at ceremonies and sacrifices occupied the greater part of the daily life of an Emperor, when he was not pursuing a favourite

90

Right : Pottery tomb models of three seated ladies playing musical instruments. T'ang Dynasty (AD 618–906)

recreation or concubine.

One of the great weaknesses of Emperor Ching and his predecessors and successors who had achieved the throne by birthright was the nature of their upbringing. Protected from the realities of life, in the Imperial Harem, the young heirs were spoiled and pampered so that later on their own whims and wishes became the most important aspects of their lives. Both Ssu-ma Ch'ien in his *Shih Chi* and Pan Ku in the *Han Shu* note that Emperor Ching was typical of this breed of self-indulgent almost whimsical rulers. And yet the administration at the time was largely successful, and for this full credit must go to the officials and the governmental hierarchy beneath the Son of Heaven.

Much of the strength of the eunuchs resulted from the weaknesses of rulers such as Ching. In order to substantiate their positions and lay claims to promotion, the eunuchs indulged the petty wishes of emperors in the face of the less agreeable but stronger and more realistic advice of the officials. The story concerning the most distinguished and able official and general of the reign, Chao Ya-fu, illustrates graphically how even dedicated servants of the state might suffer at the hands of a capricious Emperor. Chao was rewarded with the highest position in the government, Lieutenant Chancellor,

for his successful quelling of the Seven Kingdoms Rebellion. Being of a forthright and honest nature he did not always trouble to agree with and to follow slavishly the Emperor, and it happened that he was opposed to the suggestion from the Emperor's mother that the brother of the Emperor's newly adopted Empress should be made a marquis as a matter of course. The precedent for promotion to marquis, Chao said, was distinguished military service or membership of the Imperial Liu family.

Perhaps surprisingly, Emperor Ching conceded the point; he could after all claim that it was not his suggestion. But a little later the Emperor announced his decision to enfeoff five Hun kings who had surrendered to the Chinese. Chao protested in a manner bound to upset the Emperor, saying: 'These people have turned traitor to their king and have surrendered to Your Majesty. If Your Majesty makes marquises of them how will you be able to reprove your subjects who don't keep faith with you?'

Such logic was wasted on the petulant Emperor who promptly enfeoffed the Huns. Furthermore, Ching could not let such criticism pass and he resolved to settle the score with his Chancellor. He summoned Chao to the private apartments in the Palace to enjoy a feast and set before him large uncut pieces of meat and no chopsticks. With his accustomed aplomb, and not thinking of the possible implications, Chao asked the Master of the Mats to bring some chopsticks. This, of course, implied criticism of the Imperial host, and the Emperor was quick to respond, 'This too cannot be unsatisfactory to you, sir?' Chao had fallen for the ploy, and Emperor Ching merely commented, 'This man is tormented by desire . . .'.

Now it was only necessary to find some slight pretext to eliminate Chao entirely from the Imperial lists. This occurred when Chao's son purchased five hundred suits of armour from the Department of Works and the Emperor was informed. When questioned, Chao replied that these suits were burial objects, to which the questioning official's curt retort was, 'If you, sir, do not intend to rebel on earth, then you merely intend to rebel below the earth!' In spite of pressures to admit a plot, Chao steadfastly refused to succumb, fasted and died in five days.

The emperor and his Court were very involved in sacrifices and ceremony; it was clearly in their interests to foster beliefs in the favours and benefits dispensed by supernatural powers to the ruling house. An entire department of the Han government was given over to the maintenance and organisation of ceremony. Their duties included not only maintaining places of worship and ancestral shrines, but providing all the required paraphernalia, organising the Emperor's travels to holy places and sites, and supporting the entourage of priests, acolytes and musicians.

By far the most important of the emperor's religious and ceremonial activities were concerned with the worshipping of his ancestors. We have seen how at all levels of the earliest recognisable Chinese societies ancestor worship was the principal religious theme. By the Han period, Imperial ancestor worship had become a most important undertaking. Shrines were erected in all parts of the Empire, each with a complement of priests and sentinels, all of whom had to be maintained by the state. When the emperor made a journey to one of these far-flung ancestral shrines a major and expensive operation was mounted, involving the supply and organisation of transport, chariots and palanquins, guards, consorts and attendants, all of whom had to be housed and fed, together with their own slaves and servants. At the shrine itself it was customary for pigs and sheep to be sacrificed in recognition of the power and authority of the ancestor.

Of the 'holy sites' visited by the Han emperors for special ceremonies, the most important was Mount T'ai (T'ai-shan), situated in the eastern coastal province of Shantung, to the south of the present provincial capital of China. Mountains occupied a special place in Chinese mythology; they were almost deities, considered as great natural powers which acted like living beings. Thus their influence could be won by the offering of prayers and sacrifices. This veneration stemmed from the two significant functions of the mountain; first, as the stabilising force dominating and controlling the surrounding countryside – 'It prevents the ground from moving and rivers from overflowing; it opposes earthquakes and floods.' Second, the mountain was the peak around which the clouds gather to bring rain and hence fertility to the soil.

T'ai-shan, the Eastern Peak, rising to a fairly modest height of a little over eight thousand feet, is nevertheless higher than any other mountain in the east. The 'President of the East' became the most revered of the mountains in China; in the eleventh century it was promoted to a rank 'equal to Heaven'. The heaping of honours on the peak became something of a dynastic competition; in order to outbid previous distinctions, a Yüan emperor in the thirteenth century promoted the mountain to 'Emperor equal to the Sky, great giver of life, good and holy.' The later Ming emperors also exercised their imaginations in dreaming up further honours for the venerable peak.

Emperor Ching never quite made the journey to the summit of Mount T'ai. It was undoubtedly a formidable undertaking and few emperors achieved it. However, in 110 BC, the great Emperor Wu did. He was, as we have seen, a tougher and more resilient fellow than most of the Liu family. In May of that year the indefatigable Emperor ascended the mountain and performed the sacrifice of *feng* to Heaven. For the event, the altar atop the mountain was 120 feet wide and 20 feet high, with three flights of steps to ascend it. A stone slab some 31 feet high was set up to record the sacrifice and on it inscribed 'dark wine was presented and raw fish offered on the sacrificial table. The Emperor then descended the mountain and performed the sacrifice of *shan* [to the earth] at Mount Liang-fu [a lower peak on Mount T'ai] worshipping the Ruler of the Earth, to show that, "he had increased the breadth of his territory. This was an ancient institution."'

It was customary for a stele, or stone memorial tablet, such as that established by Emperor Wu in 110 BC, to be implanted in recognition of a great Imperial sacrifice on the mountain. To this day the top of Mount T'ai and the T'ai-shan Temple, originally constructed in the Han Dynasty, are dotted with such memorials.

There were other important ceremonies which demanded the attentions of the emperor, and thus the whole Imperial entourage and paraphernalia. Fertility and the soil were always to the forefront of people's minds in such an agrarian society, and the Emperor Wen remarked in an edict of 167 BC: 'By the aid of the spirits of the ancestral temples and the blessings of the altars of the soil and grain, the land within the borders is at peace and my people are without distress.' The Spirit of the Soil was worshipped at all levels of society, but the attendance of the emperor was only required when things had gone disastrously wrong, for example drought, flood or earthquake; all common occurrences in ancient China. An altar was set up wherever it was thought that the Spirit might be accessible, and great drum-beating and other rituals performed to bring him to life and fertility. If there were floods, then it was necessary to restrain him by tying a red cord round the mound associated with the Spirit's presence.

94   The more personal aspects of Han mythological and religious beliefs were

Top right : A lively and expressive pottery tomb model of an old story-teller, retrieved from a tomb near Ch'eng-tu in Szechwan province. Eastern Han Dynasty

Bottom right : A grey-green glazed pottery tomb figure of a musician with pointed headgear, playing a harp. Third–fourth centuries AD

expressed principally in the various concepts of immortality. The emperor and his Court were no less concerned with immortality and the elixir of life than the most superstitious and naïve of the peasantry. Emperor Ching was one of many who sent expeditions in search of other-worldly immortals who, it was believed, dwelt in distant regions beyond the border of the Chinese Empire. Ching's successor, the great Emperor Wu, was an even more ardent pursuer of immortality. Once an official, Kung-sun Ch'ing, reported to him that he had met a 'spirit being' at Mount Tung-lai, in Shantung province, who had expressed a wish to meet the Son of Heaven. So delighted was the Emperor that he immediately favoured Kung-sun Ch'ing with the rank of Palace Chancellor and then set off for the mountain. After a sojourn of a few days he had not succeeded in meeting the spirit but he did see the footprint of a giant man. This was sufficient to sustain hope in the Emperor, who then dispatched several thousand magicians upon another wild-goose chase to 'search for the spirits and gather the herbs of immortality'. Eventually the newly appointed Palace Chancellor was driven to all manner of wild suggestions to retain the Emperor's faith. The Chancellor advised: 'It is quite possible to meet with immortals. It is only that Your Majesty always rushes off in great haste to see them and therefore never succeeds. Now if you would only build some turrets like those in the city wall of Kou-shih and set out dried meat and jujubes, I believe the spirits could be induced to come, for they like to live in towers!' It was because of this advice that Emperor Wu gave orders for additional towers to be built in the Imperial Palace at Ch'ang-an, and also the 'Increased Life' and 'Long Life' towers at the Sweet Springs Palace.

Just as important as physical immortality was the desire for eternal bliss in some circumstances beyond the natural world and the scope of human imagination. Hence Taoist ideas of an eternal paradise ruled over by Hsi Wang-mu, the Queen Mother of the West, gained great currency and were taken up by the Imperial clan as well as the common folk.

These official and semi-official affairs took up most of the Emperor's time, and that of his close officials, advisers and retinue. When not attending to the affairs of state – either comparatively lethargically as one suspects Liu Sheng's father did, or with the restless vigour of his successor, Wu – or performing the ancestral rites or chasing some mythical aid to immortality, the Han emperors could indulge their personal pleasures. There seems to be

Right : A section of the Great Wall of China near the Nanking Gate. Originally built during the fourth and third centuries BC it was extended and consolidated by the Ch'in Emperor, Shih Huang-ti

Over : A view of the inside of the Forbidden City in Peking as it is today. Although reconstructed during the Ch'ing Dynasty, the concept of a series of audience halls with intervening courtyards is substantially the same as that of Han Dynasty palaces

a degree of consistency here. Hunting was a favourite pastime, and the Imperial interest in chasing boar or deer is reflected in Han art.

An incident between the founding Emperor Kao Tsu and his Prime Minister, Hsiao Ho, illustrates how strongly he felt about his hunting pleasures. On a journey back to Ch'ang-an from a military campaign in the west, the Emperor was besieged by petitioners along the roadside claiming that the Minister had forced them to sell their land and houses at unfair prices in order to accumulate a vast fortune for himself. Having returned to the Palace, Kao Tsu summoned Hsiao and presented the petition to him. 'I see you have been making a profit from the people', he said laughing. The Emperor then suggested that the Minister do something for them to make amends. Hsiao Ho now suggested on behalf of the people, 'The region of Chang-an is very narrow and constricted and yet there is a great deal of idle land going to waste in the Shang-lin park [the Emperor's private hunting-park]. I beg that the people be allowed to use the park for farmland, leaving the straw and other remains from their crops as fodder for beasts.' At this, the Emperor flew into a rage and retorted, 'You have succeeded in getting a lot of money and bribes from the merchants and now for their sake you want to take my park away from me.'

He promptly turned his Prime Minister over to the law officials and sent him to prison. In conversation with another palace official concerning the incident the Emperor explained his action thus: 'But now my Prime Minister has been accepting money from a lot of dirty merchants and in return asks for my park so that he can ingratiate himself with the people.' This remark also throws some light upon the official and aristocratic view of the merchant classes, who were growing both in numbers and wealth.

The Shang-lin hunting-park was formed as a pleasure place of the Han emperors. The poet Ssu-ma Hsiang-ju, who served Liu Sheng's father as a mounted guard, since the Emperor had a liking for literature, wrote on the beauty of the park and the Imperial hunting-parties:

The Son of Heaven stakes his palisades and holds his hunts,
Mounted in a carriage of carved ivory,
Drawn by six jade-spangled horses sleek as dragons,
Rainbow pennants stream before him,
Cloud banners trail in the wind,
In the vanguard ride the hide-covered carriages,

97

Top left : Terracotta tomb model of a village compound showing the small cluster of dwellings which characterised rural communities in the Han Dynasty

Bottom left : Painted pottery tomb model of tumblers, acrobats, dancers and musicians entertaining courtiers and officials, unearthed in 1969 at Chinan in Shantung province. Western Han Dynasty

Behind, the carriages of his attendants,
A coachman as clever as Sun Shu grasps the reins,
A driver as skilful as the Duke of Wei stands beside him.
His attendants fan out on all sides,
As they move into the palisade
They sound the sombre drums
And send the hunters to their posts
They corner the quarry among the rivers,
And spy them from high hills,
Then the carriages and horsemen thunder forth
Startling the heavens, shaking the earth,
Vanguard and rear dash in different directions,
Scattering after the prey
On they race in droves,
Rounding hills, streaming across the lowlands,
Like enveloping clouds of drenching rain,
Leopards and panthers they take alive
They strike down jackals and wolves,
With their hands they seize the black and tawny bears,
And with their feet they cut down the wild sheep.
Wearing pheasant-tailed caps
And breeches of white tiger skin
Under patterned tunics
They sit astride their wild horses . . .

Emperor Ching appears to have favoured many of the less demanding recreations and to some extent confined much of his pleasures to activities in the private apartments of the Palace.

We must now look at the remainder of the Han Court. The Imperial family was to a great extent dispersed in feoffs throughout the Empire. Thus Liu Sheng was sent to Hopei province, some five hundred miles away from the capital. Here in their semi-autonomous kingdoms these petty kings carried on their affairs in much the same way as the emperor in his capital. Most of the responsibility for local government lay in their hands and they therefore held the usual audiences with officials and advisers. In addition the provincial aristocracy performed similar rites and ceremonies, rode in grand carriages bedecked with fine embroidered silks, pulled by horses in full regalia with bronze and leather trappings, and lived in palaces of considerable luxury.

Right : Group of pottery tomb figures
of men playing a game of Liu-po, in
which marked bamboo sticks were
thrown like dice and entitled the player
to move his counters on the board.
Eastern Han Dynasty

In the Imperial capital itself the other principal group in the upper echelons of the hierarchy was that of the officials, the professional civil servants, who effectively ran the country. It was they who maintained the kind of semi-centralised form of government on Confucian lines which the Chinese opted for so long ago. But the restricted educational facilities made it hard to find sufficient candidates with suitable qualifications.

It was of course a Confucian concept that the highest offices in the government should go to those of proven ability and impeccable morality, not necessarily of fortunate birth. Thus the first step in the career of an official was to surmount the educational hurdle. Having either been selected or perhaps offering himself for service, the candidate would travel to the capital city where he was subjected to a number of selective processes. Both written and oral examinations were involved, generally conducted by senior civil servants, although the emperor himself did on occasions appear and question the candidates. Little is known of the precise form or content of the examinations, but certainly potential officials were expected to know and to understand the Classics as well as Confucian teachings. In addition these examinations were a test of character for, above all, the official was to be an esteemed and revered member of the hierarchy whom none of the populace at large could fault, or whose decision question.

Inevitably these were open to corruption and there are stories recorded of favoured conditions of entry for the sons of high officials; of attractive women seducing the emperor into obtaining positions for a member of their family; or even of officials purchasing their posts. But in general the system worked

and encouraged those of high principle and ability to seek posts in the government service. We have already seen that the Emperor Ching, for example, was a comparatively weak and apathetic ruler; yet the system survived and the country flourished. This reflects the contribution of the officials.

If and when a candidate was accepted into the hierarchy he would be given a post in due course, but probably only after awaiting his turn among a 'pool' of newly created officials. The government which these officials staffed was divided into two broad categories: the central and the provincial spheres. In all probability an official's first appointment would be in a provincial authority such as Liu Sheng's kingdom of Chung-shan. Early in the Han Dynasty, Kao Tsu established fifteen commanderies and ten kingdoms, but as the Empire expanded and these units were further divided among members of the enfeoffed rulers' families, so the number increased; some two hundred years later there were eighty-three commanderies and twenty kingdoms. Theoretically, the accession to the kingship of such an enfeoffment was a hereditary right, but the central government invariably manipulated the succession to suit the Imperial line or possibly to make way for a new favourite of the Court. Commanderies were ruled over by appointed officials and were thus less bound by hereditary ties. Both units further divided into prefectures, these approximately the size of an English county, and then subdivided into wards and districts which would have approximated to an English rural or urban district. The lowest level of government was the ward, a subdivision of the district. Officials, or *Chün-tzu*, from the central government were appointed to the higher posts in local authority, while local personnel not as fully trained in the Classics and Confucianism as their masters filled the more lowly posts. The officials' functions in the provincial government were principally concerned with the raising of revenue through taxes, paid either in cash or in produce such as grain or bolts of silk. They were also responsible for the maintenance of law and order, the upkeep of communication systems, and the conscription of personnel for the army and forced labour gangs.

In the court of a provincial king, such as Liu Sheng's Court at Man-ch'eng, the officials were responsible for the maintenance of ritual and ceremony, the review and promulgation of edicts and the running of the household – functions which prepared them for their ultimate goal; service in the central administration at Ch'ang-an. One other important aspect of the provincial officials' work concerned the organisation and maintenance of

100

Right : Pottery tomb figure of a dancing lady entertaining her masters.
T'ang Dynasty (AD 618–906)

communications. Bedevilled by vast distances and difficult terrain, the communications system of ancient China was a constant worry to the government of the day, especially to one which based its daily functioning on the power and control of the central authority. Staging-posts were established along routes throughout the Empire, each staffed by grooms and extra horses. Messengers from the seat of power in Ch'ang-an would ride continually, using refreshed horses at each post.

Naturally it was the aim of every ambitious official to obtain a position at the Han capital. The system allowed for steady promotion through the ranks and dedicated service was usually rewarded, although the intrigues of officials to gain favours and to improve their lot nearly match those of the Imperial family itself. They lived in circumstances far beyond those of the average people, even if posted to a remote authority, perhaps in Chinese Turkestan or in the southern coastal provinces. Their way of life was not quite that of the Imperial family but was certainly matched only by the wealthiest of merchants, who, of course, could not command the same dignity and respect. A visitor to a prominent local official or a member of the central government would enter the residence, often his office as well, through an imposing gateway and into a large courtyard flanked by the apartments of the official's staff. Through inner courtyards were the private rooms and halls of the master and his family. All this was carefully planned to play its part in the maintenance of order and the hierarchy, to increase the dignity of the official in such imposing and placid surroundings and to make the humble petitioner even more aware of his lowly station in life.

On any occasion, when either receiving visitors or paying homage to a higher ranking member of the government, the official would wear his full regalia, in the first case to impress upon those below him the dignity of his person and position, and in the second case in deference to those above him. These consisted of full robes of fine silk, with voluminous sleeves, the ornate hat appropriate to his rank, and a belt of leather often clasped with a rich and beautiful belt-hook of bronze, possibly inlaid with gold, silver or turquoise. He would probably hold a jade sceptre as the symbol of his office, and wear the appropriate seals and ribbons. When visiting the emperor his carriage or palanquin would set him down at the gate of the Palace, and with a great show of enthusiasm and zeal the official would run to the hall in which he was to have his audience. At all levels the attention to such ceremonial was strictly adhered to in order to maintain the vast and complex hierarchy. The pupils and servants of the officials showed to their masters the same kind of courtly respect that the master showed to the emperor.

The structure of the government itself reflects the order so inherent in Han society. The provincial government was, as we have seen, broken down into comparatively small organs of local power and authority. The central government had far wider responsibilities and the organisation was much like that in Britain today. At the top were the two most senior officials whose offices roughly correspond to those of a prime minister and head of the civil service. These men had the closest contacts with the emperor, were generally in his confidence and were indeed powerful figures. Chou Ya-fu, the Chancellor or equivalent of the head of the civil service at the time of Liu Sheng, was held in awe by even the enfeoffed vassal lords and kings. Ssu-ma Ch'ien records that 'during the reign of the Emperor Ching, whenever there was some important matter to be discussed at court, none of the marquises dared to try to stand on an equal footing with Chou Ya-fu . . .'.

Beneath these two immensely influential figures, men nonetheless of possibly humble origins, who had attained their positions through education, study and devotion to duty, there were nine principal ministries. The purely administrative ministries were divided into those responsible for justice and punishment (the principal forms of punishment were tattooing, cutting off the nose and cutting off the heel), receipt of tribute from foreign kings and rulers (a particularly relevant ministry during the expansionist years of the Han Dynasty), collection of revenue, and major work projects. Other ministries were concerned with aspects of the Imperial Court and household: dealing with religious ceremony and rituals, maintenance of the Imperial palaces and establishments throughout the Empire, regulation of enfeoffments and the Imperial records, observation of the stars, and the control and administration of the Imperial guards and armies. The armies were constantly expanding during the Han period, and conscription in the form of a two-year service was even introduced at one stage in order to combat the Hsiung-nu and to expand the Imperial frontiers.

Life at a Court of the Han Dynasty at the time of Prince Liu Sheng, or in a provincial capital, was beset by intrigue and overshadowed by the possibility of sudden and violent revenge or death. But as compensation the members of the Imperial family and of the official classes enjoyed a life of immense luxury in dire contrast to the meagre lives of the population at large. Not for them the profusion of fine silk embroideries and woven damasks, the silk-lined leather shoes, robes of silk trimmed with sable and ornamented with duck plumes, or the jewellery of gold, silver and jade. The extravagance of those in high positions extended to all aspects of life. Their meals were veritable banquets, of game, fish, roasts, kid, quail, and other delicacies garnished with all manner of seasonings and relishes. Whilst Prince Liu Sheng and his guests savoured such delights they would be entertained by musicians; all Imperial, aristocratic and even official households maintained their own orchestras. Or perhaps they may have watched performing tigers, foreign dancing-girls or the traditional acrobats and jugglers, still a favourite entertainment in China.

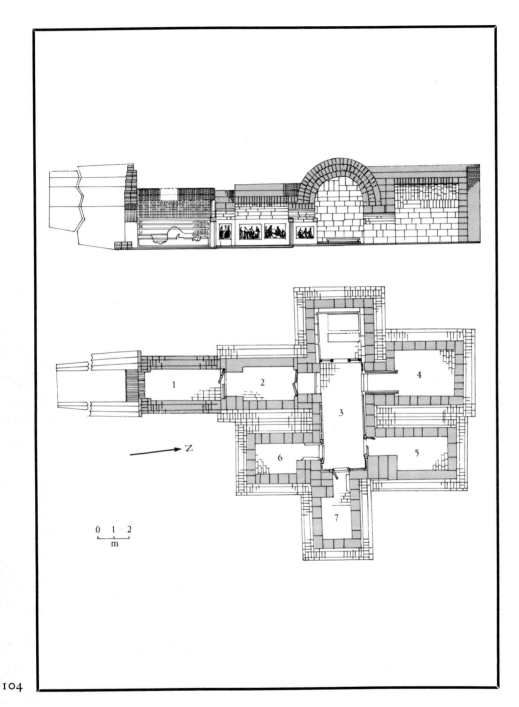

Above : Plan and cross-section of a large brick-vaulted tomb recently discovered at Mi-hsien in Honan province. The walls were painted with secular scenes from the life of the departed

Right The entrance to the tomb of the Ming Emperor Wan Li (reigned 1573–1620), near Peking. The design is basically the same as that used in the royal tombs of the Shang Dynasty at Anyang, some three thousand years earlier

The demise of members of the Court, whether Imperial or official, was accompanied by equal ceremony and extravagance. The form of Prince Liu Sheng's tomb and that of the Princess Tou Wan, like a 'stretched' cruciform, was the norm. The ceremony itself was a lengthy affair, accompanied by all the pomp and paraphernalia that one associates with the royal burials of ancient Egypt. By the Han period the practice of human or animal sacrifice had died out and in its place the dead were provided with all the material necessities and comforts he or she might need in the after-life. The contents of Prince Liu Sheng's tomb illustrates this principle and we have seen there how much time, trouble and wealth was expended.

We can imagine the great procession: headed by the 'spirits that clear the way', followed by guards, attendants, courtiers and mourners, all in their full ceremonial costume, their long richly woven or embroidered silk robes, jade, gold and silver jewellery, with brightly painted banners fluttering; then the funeral carriage itself, pulled either by funeral horses with bronze and lacquer fittings, or by the slaves and servants of the dead king, and decorated with silks and the badges and symbols of the dead man's rank. Following this procession came the carriages containing all those material goods and possessions which it was thought that the dead man would require in the hereafter, ranging from the magnificent bronze ritual vessels we have seen from our Prince's tomb, to little boxes, either bronze, silver or lacquer, containing food.

The body itself was generally laid out in specially prepared silk robes, like that of the wife of the Marquis Li Tsang, discovered in 1972 at Mawangtui near Ch'ang-sha in Hunan, which was wrapped in no fewer than twenty layers of the finest woven and embroidered silks. It is because silk robes were the general rule that the jade suits of Prince Liu Sheng and Princess Tou Wan are so exceptional.

6 EVERYDAY LIFE IN HAN CHINA

THROUGHOUT THEIR LIVES THE HAN IMPERIAL FAMILY, THE aristocracy and the officials were surrounded by the luxury of riches that was the lot of the privileged classes in ancient China. But they formed only a tiny portion of the population, at that time conservatively estimated to be approximately sixty million persons. The lives and conditions of the common folk provide a stark contrast with those of their masters.

Apart from those employed in the households or armies of the emperor, kings, nobles and officials, or in the occasional urban industries, such as chariot and carriage construction, the lives of the people of Han lay in the countryside. There were cities, such as Ch'ang-an and Loyang (the capital city of the Later [or Eastern] Han period), but it is estimated that the rural population outnumbered the urban population by a factor of ten to one.

Even the Emperor recognised the importance of agriculture and the contribution of the peasantry. In the summer of 167 BC the Emperor Wen announced: 'Agriculture is the foundation of the world. No duty is greater.' He was probably among the most sympathetic of the Han rulers, and certainly more so than Liu Sheng's father, the Emperor Ching, who expressed little interest in or concern for the common people. Wen continued his edict: 'Now if anyone follows this [agricultural] pursuit diligently he still has to pay the impositions of land tax and tax on the produce. This is making no distinction between what is fundamental and what is least important. This is not appropriate to our way of encouraging agriculture. Let there be abolished the land tax and tax on produce, and let their be granted to the orphans and widows of the Empire, cloth, silk, and silk padding to each person a certain amount.'

But Emperor Wen's humane edict did not substantially alter the lives and conditions of the rural peasantry. They lived, not in the elegant multi-storeyed pavilions of the noblemen, but in huts of mud and straw with thatched roofs and beaten earth floors. To combat ever-present natural disasters, such as floods or droughts, and perhaps the harsh treatment of landlords or the destruction caused by contending armies, farm and household units often combined to form what in modern terms might be called a co-operative. Since farm produce formed the basic revenue of the state such an organisation also benefited the government in the collection of taxes.

Most of what we know of the life of the country peasant in ancient China is gleaned from pictorial representations, scenes of rural activities depicted on

Previous page : Pottery tomb model of a sty and pig. Eastern Han Dynasty

Right : Rubbing of a Han stone relief showing three peasant farmers hoeing the land

tomb reliefs or the stamped clay bricks and tiles ornamenting the burial chambers of their masters. The Chinese histories which tell us of the lives of Prince Liu Sheng and his family say nothing of the peasants over whom they ruled. They do, however, tell us something of the tenure of the land tilled by the peasants. In some cases they owned the land they worked, but generally they were tenant-farmers working land owned by the enfeoffed masters and paying taxes to them in the form of produce.

In the north of China, on the plains of the Yellow River, often described as the cradle of Chinese civilisation, the farmers' principal product was grain, either wheat or millet. Their daily life was simple, hard and probably not very rewarding; a repetitive existence of ploughing, sowing, hoeing and harvesting. A relief brick excavated at Ch'eng-tu, the capital city of Szechwan province in the west of China, captures entirely the daily routine of the Han countryman. In the lower picture two men reap the grain with their scythes, while three others seem to be gathering the harvest. On the left a sixth figure enters the scene carrying what is probably food and sustenance for the reapers. In the scene above hunters aim their bows at the geese flying overhead as they sit beside a pool abundant with fish.

Ploughing and hoeing were generally done by sheer manpower, but oxen and bullocks were also used. A carved stone relief from a tomb in Shensi province, dated 107 AD, depicts a ploughing scene with two bullocks pulling the plough. This type of machine, like most at the time, was made of wood but iron implements were being introduced towards the end of the Dynasty.

The second major product was hemp, for the coarse cloth which clothed most of the people. The pictures of the reapers and the ploughman show that the usual costume of the people was a roughly knee-length outer robe or coat, belted at the waist. So far as one can tell from fragmented paintings and reliefs these were generally in a plain drab colour, in striking contrast to the rich silk robes of the nobles and officials. Similarly, the food of the common people was simple fare based on the staple product of the land and water; grain, millet, rice (in the south) and fish.

We know little of village life in the rural areas at the time but it seems likely to have continued the pattern set by the communities of the Neolithic period. Thus the village would be formed by clusters of small houses round a larger communal building. Pottery tomb models indicate the style of architecture. Usually the small enclave encompassed a courtyard or animal pen, while the house itself was a rectangular building, sometimes with a tile roof. This was certainly not always the case and many peasant houses would have been less resilient structures of mud and straw lathe applied round wooden pillars, and with a thatch roof. Inside the house – if pottery tomb models are any guide – we can assume that the stove was the most important feature of the household. Many of these strange-looking rectangular blocks, with relief-moulded images of fish or animal heads on the top surface, have been retrieved from Han tombs across China.

There were a number of public buildings in each community and – again on the evidence of tomb models – the granary must have been the one most important to the people. Certainly the grain store played a significant role in an agriculturally dependent community liable to suffer from natural disasters which might seriously affect the crop. Tomb reliefs also illustrate grain-milling procedures, with a well-organised arrangement suggesting that this also was often a communal or village responsibility.

Another constant problem facing the countrymen was the provision of water; often a case of far too little, or far too much. This too became some-

110 thing of a communal undertaking and the pottery models of well-heads which

Right : Pottery tomb model of a village compound showing houses and farm buildings, including a pig sty in the foreground. Excavated at Cheng-chou in Honan province. Eastern Han Dynasty

are another feature of Han burial sites suggest a scale that was certainly beyond the individual peasant farmer. Similarly, the provision and maintenance of irrigation ditches, preventing floods and watering the fields, was generally a communal, even national, undertaking.

While the peasant farmers were tied to labouring on the land, raising produce and stock, particularly sheep, cattle and pigs, there began to emerge the inevitable middle-men, the merchants. Although they played a vital role in the distribution of produce and merchandise they were nevertheless seen as exploiters of the people and, in a sense, usurpers of the power and control of the government and officials. The story of the Jen family shows how ordinary people of guile and wit were able to become wealthy, even though they were neither noblemen nor officials.

Their story is related by Ssu-ma Ch'ien, writing at the time of the Emperor Wu.

Rubbing taken from a relief-moulded brick from a tomb near Ch'eng-tu in Szechwan. In the upper picture, archers point their bows at flying birds, whilst seated beside a pool well stocked with fish; in the lower picture har- *vesters are at work. Eastern Han Dynasty*

When the Ch'in Dynasty was overthrown and the leaders of the revolt were all scrambling for gold and jewels, Mr Jen quietly dug a hole and stored away the grain that had been in his charge. Later, when the armies of Chu and Han were stalemated at Jung-yang and the people were unable to plough their fields and plant their crops, the price of grain rose to ten thousand cash a picul and all the gold and jewels of the great leaders soon found their way into the hands of Mr Jen. This was the start of the Jen family fortune. But while other rich people were outdoing each other in luxurious living, the Jen family lived frugally and devoted all their energies to farming and raising animals. And while most people tried to buy the cheapest fields and pasture lands, the Jen family bought up only those that were really valuable and of good quality. Thus the family remained wealthy for several generations.

There were also growing numbers of people employed in semi-industrial enterprises, which were often developed and managed by independent entrepreneurs. Iron-smelting was fast becoming an established industry, especially as agricultural techniques developed and the demand for more sophisticated machinery increased. Again it was the ingenuity and enterprise of the common folk that promoted much of this industry. One such was Mr Cho, whose family were captured by the Ch'in and removed from their homeland to what he described as 'a region too narrow and barren'. He asked to be sent to Mount Min where 'there are fertile plains full of edible tubers so that one may live all his life without suffering from famine. The people there are clever at commerce and make their living by trade.' His request to be sent to a distant region was granted and he was ordered to move, not to Mount Min, but to Lin-ch'iung. This pleased him greatly for when he got there he found a mountain which yielded iron, which he began to smelt and 'lay other plans to accumulate wealth'. Soon he dominated trade among the people of Tien and Shu districts. Thus he 'grew so rich that he owned a thousand young slaves, and the pleasures he indulged in among his fields and lakes and on his bird and animal hunts were like those of a great lord'. Mr Cho was a success, and the description of his leisure-time pursuits surely matches, or nearly matches, those of Prince Liu Sheng and his aristocratic colleagues.

Such stories are, however, very much the exception for the wealth of Han China lay for the most part in the hands of the Imperial hierarchy and the officials. The Court at Ch'ang-an soon became aware of this growing merchant or 'industrialist' class; however few they might be, their control of certain raw materials and production, and their accumulation of wealth posed a threat 113 to the Imperial clan. In any event the Imperial Court considered that any profits and fortunes that ensued should come to them; it was not the function of the people to amass wealth. So the government decreed what was a virtual monopoly over the two basic raw materials, iron and salt, thereby destroying the threat of private enterprise becoming a significant factor in the economic development of the Han.

Above : Drawing of a stone relief from a tomb in Shensi, dated AD 107, depicting a ploughing scene in Han China

Left : A scene in modern China near Hangchow

Matters came to a head during the adventurous years of Emperor Wu's reign when the Han armies were undertaking ambitious campaigns involving vast expense. With the government treasuries fast becoming depleted, two assistants to the Minister of Agriculture presented the following decree to the Emperor:

Mountains and seas are the storehouses of heaven and earth, and it is proper that any revenue from them should go to the privy treasure of the Son of Heaven. Your Majesty, however, being of an unselfish nature, has turned over the control of these natural resources to the Ministry of Agriculture to supplement the income from taxes. We propose, therefore, that the manufacture of salt be permitted to any of the common people who are willing to supply their own capital and agree to use implements furnished by the government. Evaporating-pans will be rented to them by the officials. At present there are people with no fixed residence or occupation who attempt without authority to gain control of the resources of the

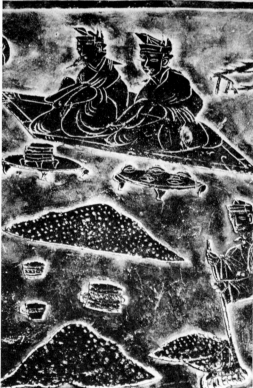

A series of stone reliefs from a tomb near Nanking, illustrating everyday village and farm life in Han China, and focusing on the provision and preparation of food

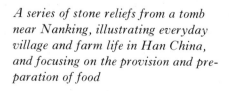

mountains and seas, accumulating enormous fortunes and exploiting the poor. Countless proposals have already been made on ways to prevent this situation. We suggest that anyone who dares to cast his own iron vessels and engage in the evaporation of salt be condemned to wear fetters on his left foot, and that his vessels and other equipment be confiscated by the government. In the provinces, which do not produce iron, sub-offices for the control of iron goods should be set up, subject for convenience sake to the jurisdiction of the district in which they are located.

The plan was put into immediate effect and the wealthy men who had previously owned and managed the iron and salt industries were made officials in charge of the local government bureau set up to handle these affairs. This move might possibly have had more serious repercussions than in fact it did, for as a result, merchants actually managed to become government officials. This represented a development which, had it been permitted

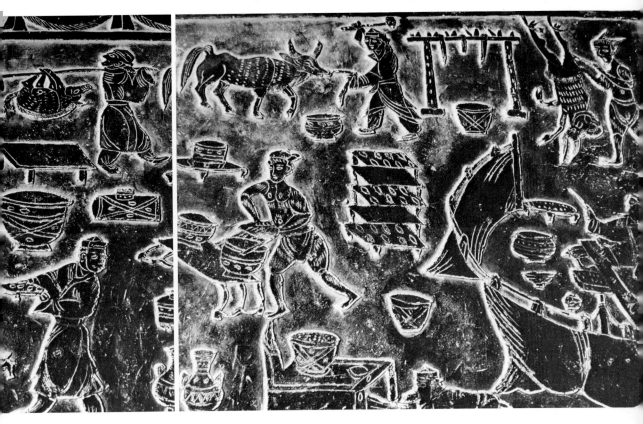

to continue, could have undermined the basic Confucian quality of the Han administration. As it happened, their merchant's acumen never left them as the Grand Historian, Ssu-ma Ch'ien, wrote at the time of Emperor Wu: 'The merchants, taking advantage of the frequent changes of currency, had been hoarding goods in order to make a profit.' As a result of this tendency, further edicts followed demanding more taxes on the merchants and restricting their activities within the official hierarchy.

The common people were also used in the immense public work projects which were undertaken during the Han Dynasty. Underpinning this period of great territorial expansion and of economic and technical development was a system of forced labour. Based on the registers of households returned by local officials the system demanded that all males – except, of course, members of the Imperial household, nobles and officials – should do one month's service in the state labour corps every year, starting at the age of twenty-three and ending at the age of fifty-six.

The government projects included the building of roads, canals, palaces and Imperial tombs. The tombs of Prince Liu Sheng and Princess Tou Wan would have been hollowed out of the hard rock by such gangs of men. Indeed

118

Above : Pottery tomb model of a mastiff-type dog.
Opposite top left : Pottery tomb model of a granary. Eastern Han Dynasty
Top right : Pottery tomb model of a well-head. Han Dynasty

Bottom left : The top of a bronze cowrie-container, excavated at Shih-chai-shan in Yunnan province. Western Han Dynasty
Bottom right : Pottery tomb model of a sheep-pen. Eastern Han Dynasty

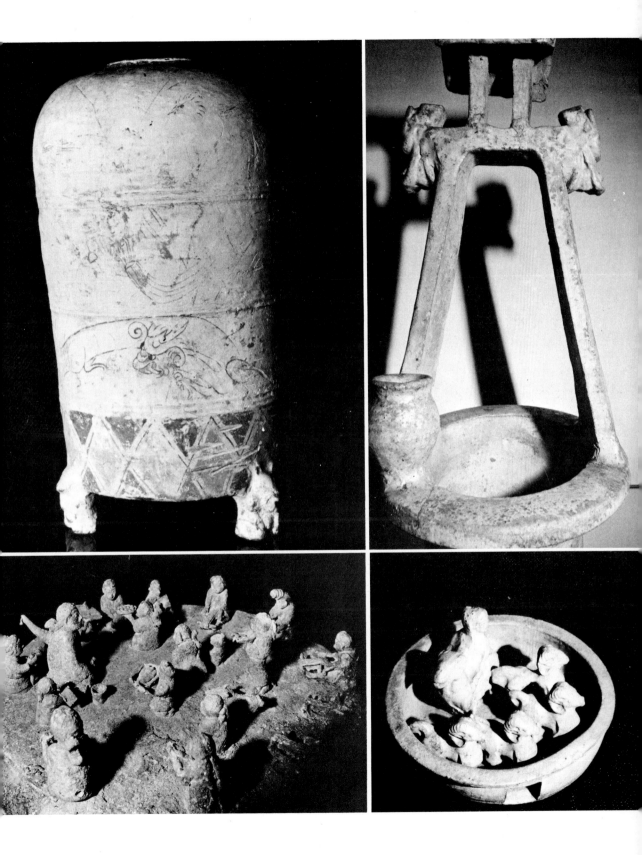

all the rich and varied works of art that have been retrieved from those tombs, the bronze vessels, jade carvings, pottery vessels and woven and embroidered silks were made by artisan craftsmen working in state workshops in the service of the hierarchy. Gangs of forced labour were also employed on the construction of the Great Wall, in addition to the three hundred thousand soldiers and all the criminals in the land who, it is said, were put to the task. The scale of the operation and the difficulties involved in supporting such a vast body of men working in inaccessible territory is illustrated by the report that of 182 loads of grain dispatched only one would arrive, the rest being eaten or sold *en route*.

A typical enterprise involving the forced labour gangs was the building of a canal, early in the reign of Emperor Wu during the second century BC, to transport grain. The current Minister of Agriculture, Cheng Tang-shih, informed the Emperor:

Up to now grain from east of the Pass has been brought to the capital by being transported up the Wei River. The operation requires six months to complete and the course is over nine hundred *li* [approximately three hundred miles] and beset with dangerous places. Now if we were to dig a canal from the Wei River beginning

Above : Relief-moulded brick from a tomb at Yang-tzu-shan, near Ch'eng-tu, in Szechwan province, showing the manufacture of salt. Brine was dredged up from the well and the water then evaporated. Additional interest is pro- *vided by the deer-hunt, which is shown taking place in the top right of the picture. Eastern Han Dynasty*

at Ch'ang-an and following along the Southern Mountains to the Yellow River, the distance could be reduced to something over three hundred *li*. We would have a much easier route for transporting grain, and the trip could be accomplished in three months. Morever, the people living along the canal could utilise the water to irrigate over ten thousand *ch'ing* [a *ch'ing* is approximately 16·5 acres] of farmland. Thus we could reduce the time and labour required to haul grain and at the same time increase the fertility of the lands within the Pass and obtain a higher yield.

It is then recorded that a force of twenty to thirty thousand men dug the canal. The project took three years to complete. Throughout Chinese history such projects have been undertaken, employing enormous armies of men, and even today vast resources of manpower remain fundamental to the Chinese economy and industry.

River- or canal-borne traffic provided one of the most important means of communication and transport in early China, indeed many of the canals built in the distant past, during the Han, T'ang, Sung and Ming Dynasties are still in use today. Even the vessels themselves seem to have changed little. The long, narrow boats of the Han Dynasty, with small living quarters, bear a striking resemblance to those now chugging in convoy along the canals of China. Most of those operating today are motor-powered and perhaps the

121

Drawing of a rubbing taken from a stone relief of a Han Dynasty tomb in Kiangsu province, one of the most important silk-producing areas of China. In this weaving-shed, a primitive type of draw-loom is illustrated

cargoes differ, but the system is essentially the same and the waterways are still fully exploited.

It was not always so easy to undertake great works of public utility, for often it was thought such schemes might tamper with the ways of nature. Around 130 BC, the Yellow River broke its banks and flooded the surrounding countryside, a not unfamiliar occurrence in China before the complex systems of drainage, many only recently completed, were instituted. The Emperor Wu ordered its immediate repair by the forced labour gangs, but the Chancellor, T'ien Fen, advised: 'Breaks in the banks of the Yangtze and the Yellow River are all the work of Heaven. It is no easy task to stop up such breaks forcibly by human labour, and indeed to do so would hardly be in accord with the will of Heaven.'

The role of women in ancient China is difficult to determine. In the Imperial household and those of the aristocracy and the nobles they lived in pampered, but severely restricted, luxury and seldom played any significant public role in society. But we have already seen evidence of their involvement in the manœuvrings behind the scenes. We do not know whether the peasant

woman was equipped with similar abilities for handling intrigues, or indeed was ever presented with the opportunity for using them. In the Court the situation was greatly influenced by two factors; first, the women's habit of outliving their husbands, so that their sons inherited the father's position while the mother was still alive; second, the general Confucian ethic of filial piety, whereby children must show to their parents the greatest respect and obedience. Thus we find the curious case of a Han emperor deferring a reply to the advice of his counsellors on the grounds that 'I will have first to ask my mother'. The marriage of a noble girl was frequently a quasi-diplomatic manœuvre, and we shall find examples of daughters of the Imperial house being offered as 'tribute' to the Hsiung-nu. Within the Middle Kingdom such marriages were often arranged to maintain old alliances or to promote new ones between feudal or enfeoffed families. Once married, the woman's obedience to the lord of the household was paramount and thus, to a considerable extent, her filial piety duties diminished. It was only later in life, as a mother, when she herself became the object of filial piety, that the woman regained some of her former prestige. Girls in ancient China were not trained to take part in public life or war, but for service, labour and

123

Left : Rubbing taken from a Han Dynasty stone relief, illustrating silk-spinning

Above : Sorting cocoons in a modern silk factory in Wushi, one of the most important silk-producing centres in Kiangsu province

attendance in the women's apartments.

Probably the strength of family and matriarchal ties in the peasant communities was very nearly as strong, but the conditions and situations of their lives demanded a more positive contribution from the womenfolk. Apart from the obvious duties of looking after and maintaining the household, the women were widely employed in the ever-developing silk industry. According to the rules of husbandry set down late in the Han Dynasty by Ts'ui Shih, a one-time wealthy landowner who experienced bitter poverty, it was a prime function of the women to nurture the silk-worms and to keep a watchful eye over their life cycle. Then in the sixth month they would be spinning textiles, and later in the summer their tasks included washing old clothes and making new ones. Later in the year, in the autumn months, they should be employed on working hemp and making sandals.

The rules of nature and the ever-present hierarchy imposed upon the people of Han China an almost inflexible way of life. Only those semi-nomadic peoples in the north and the west, tending their herds of sheep, goats, cattle or horses, were able to exercise much independence in their daily life.

Previous page : Although generally motorised, some water-borne traffic in modern China relies on the sail. Boats on Lake T'ai in southern Kiangsu province
Above left : Pottery tomb model of a

boat, found near Canton, typical of the type which plied the waterways of Han China. Above right : The waterways of modern China are still used as a vital means of communication and transport. A busy canal scene at Wushi

7 HAN IMPERIALISM: China and the West

BY THE TIME THE PRESENT EMPEROR [EMPEROR WU, SUCCESSOR TO PRINCE Liu Sheng's father] had been on the throne a few years, a period of over seventy years had passed since the founding of the Han. During that time the nation had met with no major disturbances so that, except in times of flood or drought, every person was well supplied and every family had enough to get along on. The granaries in the cities and the countryside were full and the government treasuries were running over with wealth. In the capital the strings of cash had been stacked up by the hundreds of millions until the cords that bound them had rotted away and they could no longer be counted. In the central granary of the government, new grain was heaped on top of the old until the building was full and the grain overflowed and piled up outside, where it spoiled and became unfit to eat. Horses were to be seen in the streets and lanes of the common people or plodding in great numbers along the paths between fields, and anyone so poor as to have to ride a mare was disdained by his neighbours and not allowed to join the gatherings of the villagers. Even the keepers of the community gates ate fine grain and meat. The local officials remained at the same posts, long enough to see their sons and grandsons grow to manhood and the higher officials occupied the same positions so long that they adopted their official titles as surnames. As a result men had a sense of self-respect and regarded it as a serious matter to break the law. Their first concern was to act in accordance with what was right and to avoid shame and dishonour.

This rosy picture of Han China was written by Ssu-ma Ch'ien. And even though he may himself have been overcome by the general wealth around him at the time, and painted the life of the peasant farmer in over-enthusiastic terms, it was the undoubted wealth of Han China that financed the expansion of her borders. The map showing the borders of the Chinese Empire during the Ch'in Dynasty and *circa* 100 AD illustrates just how emphatic this expansion was.

When Kao Tsu finally defeated the Ch'in and established his Han Dynasty in 206 BC, he inherited a nation ravaged by war and the excesses of Ch'in rule. His main concern, therefore, was to consolidate his position and that of his Dynasty within the Empire. He could not afford to adopt anything more than a passive policy towards China's neighbours.

We have read constantly of the threat of the Hsiung-nu Tartars, the nomadic peoples of Turkish stock inhabiting the steppe lands of Mongolia and parts of Central Asia. Their marauding of the Chinese border territories was a constant threat to Kao Tsu, especially as it often happened that local Chinese kings and nobles were coerced into forming alliances with the Huns. For example, the *Han Shu* records:

128

Right : Detail of the head of a pottery tomb model of a lady, which again shows the sensitivity of the Han crafts-man. This figure is made of earthen-ware, covered with a white slip and was originally painted

Previous page : Rubbing of a Han stone relief showing a fleet horse-borne archer

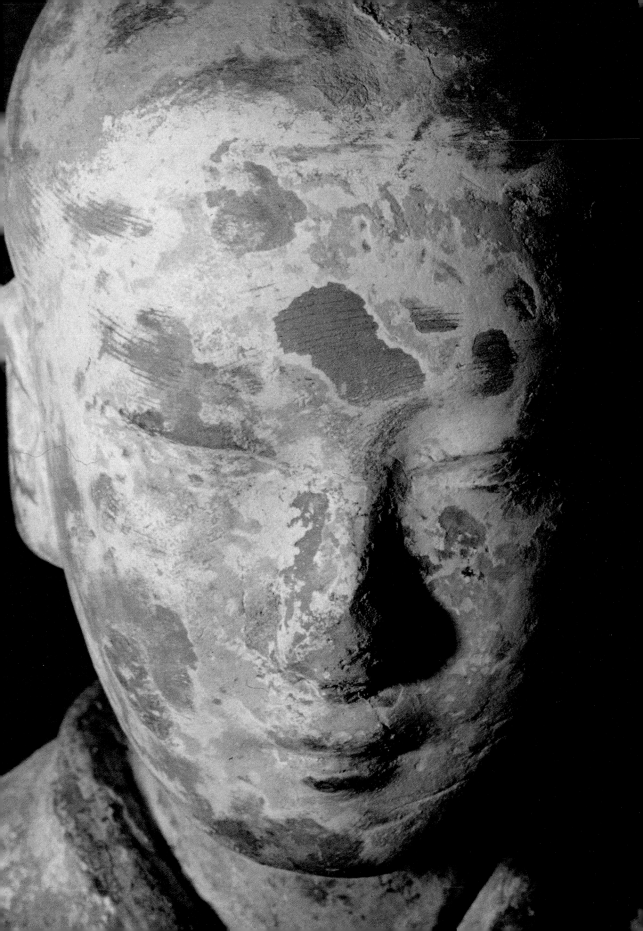

In the seventh year [of Kao Tsu's reign, 200 BC], the Hsiung-nu attacked Hsin, the King of Han, at Ma-i. Hsin joined with them in plotting a revolt in T'ai-yüan. His generals, Man-ch'iu Ch'en of Po-t'u and Wang Huang, set up Chou Li, a descendant of the royal family of Chao, as king of Chou in revolt against the Emperor. Kao Tsu in person led a force to attack them, but he encountered such severe cold that two or three out of every ten of his soldiers lost their fingers from frostbite. At last he reached P'ing-ch'eng, where the Hsiung-nu surrounded him. After seven days of siege they finally withdrew.

Because of his great military ability, sufficient indeed to defeat the Ch'in, Kao Tsu found it necessary to lead the military himself. Generally it was unusual for an emperor to take such a significant role.

Having finally extinguished the threat of King Hsin's rebels and their Hsiung-nu companions, Kao Tsu returned to the capital at Ch'ang-an in 199 BC. Meanwhile, his Prime Minister, Hsiao Ho, had been busy erecting government buildings and palaces on a scale that the Emperor considered excessive. Ssu-ma Ch'ien records: 'When Kao Tsu returned from his expedition and saw the magnificence of the palaces and its towers, he was extremely angry. "The Empire is still in great turmoil", he said to Hsiao Ho, "and though we have toiled in battle these several years, we cannot tell yet whether we will achieve final success. What do you mean by constructing palaces like this on such an extravagant scale?"' Kao Tsu's attitude to his newly founded Empire was strictly practical.

Although avoiding military action whenever possible, Kao Tsu did not shrink in the face of the enemy. If the Hsiung-nu ventured into Han territory then he met force with force. Not so his successor, the Emperor Wen. Of him Ssu-ma Ch'ien notes: 'In his relations with the Hsiung-nu tribes, as well as with recalcitrant kings of his own family, he declined the use of force whenever possible, preferring to buy peace from the Hsiung-nu with tribute and to attempt to reform his kinsmen by leniency and gentle reprimand.'

Emperor Wen tried earnestly to achieve a peaceful settlement with the Huns. In an edict of 162 BC he regretted 'that we have been unable to extend the influence of our virtues to distant regions . . . hence we have sent envoys in rapid succession, so that the cape and carriage coverings of one caravan were in sight of the second, and their wheel tracks were uninterrupted in the road, in order to enlighten the Shan-yü concerning our intentions'. The edict continues in a conciliatory tone and suggests that an entente with the Shan-yü was in fact arranged, for it concludes: 'The peace and friendship has

*Left : Pottery tomb figure of an enter-
tainer. Western Han Dynasty*

been fixed upon to begin from the present year.'

It was, however, a brittle peace. In the winter of 159 BC the *Han Shu* records: 'In the sixth year, in the winter, Hun horsemen entered the Yün-chung commandery.' The old conflict was once again reborn, the fragile peace having lasted but two years. In spite of this setback Wen maintained a passive attitude and continued to buy peace whenever possible.

His successor, the Emperor Ching, was no more a warrior than Wen himself. By all accounts Prince Liu Sheng, like his father, was also a man who preferred not to get involved in military conflicts. Apart from purchasing peace with the Hsiung-nu through presenting tribute, Emperor Ching also adopted the tactic of offering feoffdoms. In the spring of 147 BC, two Hun kings appeared with their followers at the Han border and surrendered. Ching rewarded them with territories in the Chinese Empire and enfeoffed them as marquises.

All this was a negative approach to the problem of the Hsiung-nu, and one that was soon to be reversed. The first sixty years of Han rule had been a period of consolidation and, apart from the founding Emperor Kao Tsu, the Han Imperial line had been a passive lot. The formidable, dynamic and ambitious Emperor Wu changed all that. The opening statement of the Basic Annals of Emperor Wu included in the *Han Shu* begins: 'When the fifth ruler came to the throne and began his reign in the era *Ch'ien-yüan* the Han Dynasty reached its height and glory. He drove back the barbarian tribes beyond the borders, and within the country put the laws and regulations into order.'

To begin with, Wu adopted a conciliatory attitude, offering daughters of the Imperial house to the Shan-yü, and presents of gold, silk and ornamental embroidery. But it was all in vain, as an edict issued in the spring of 133 BC records: 'The Shan-yü has treated our commands with increasing disrespect, he has invaded and pillaged our borders unceasingly. The border regions have suffered great injury from him.' Subsequently, on the advice of his counsellors, Wu mounted his first notable assault on the Hsiung-nu. A force of no less than three hundred thousand soldiers left the capital to attack the Shan-yü. They encamped in a ravine at Ma-yi, intending to lure the barbarian leader and his forces into a trap. The plot failed, the Shan-yü escaped and the massive Chinese army returned empty-handed. General Wang Hui who was responsible for the campaign 'was sentenced for having been the first to

130

Top right: Detail of the back of a bronze mirror showing an archer on horseback. The full-stretch gallop expresses the preoccupation of Han artists with lively naturalism. First century AD

Bottom right: Bronze crossbow trigger mechanism of the type used by the Han armies in their Central Asian campaigns. This example is dated in the inscription to the third year of Chien-an, AD 198

plan the campaign but not having advanced it, he was sent to prison and died'. Such was the price of failure under Emperor Wu.

The Huns continued to raid the border and to pillage Chinese territory, but all the while Han was growing richer and stronger. The vast resources of manpower made available by the forced labour system were increasingly being put to military use. Skirmishing along the border increased daily and the loss of life, on both sides, was enormous. Entry after entry in the Han history records such incidents as, in 125 BC, 'In the summer the Huns entered Tai, Ting-hsiang and Shang commanderies, killing and kidnapping several thousand persons.' In the very next year, 'The General-in-Chief, Wei Ch'ing, leading six generals and more than one hundred thousand troops, went out of Kao-ch'üeh and So-fang commanderies and took fifteen thousand heads and captives.'

Gradually the Chinese pressure began to tell and they ventured further beyond the Great Wall, into the Ordos region of modern Inner Mongolia, and westwards towards the Gobi Desert. The scale of the wars increased as the Han gained ascendancy. One of the most significant campaigns was that undertaken in 119 BC by the illustrious General-in-Chief, Wei Ch'ing, and the 'Swift Cavalry General', Ho Ch'ü-ping. Wei was the offspring of an illicit relationship between a clerk in the office of the Marquis of Ping-yang and one of the concubines, a certain Dame Wei. After serving as a lowly shepherd boy, he managed to become a rider in the Marquis' household and then rapidly worked his way up the ranks. Ho Ch'ü-ping was the son of Wei Ch'ing's older sister, who at the tender age of twenty or so was leading a force of 'eight hundred of the fastest and most daring riders'. Both were to play a vital role in the expansion of the Chinese Empire.

The joint forces of Wei and Ho, amounting to one hundred thousand cavalrymen and several hundred thousand foot soldiers, left to seek out the Huns in the Gobi Desert. Wei reached the north side of the desert, probably in the region of the present Russian-Mongolian borders, where he surrounded the Shan-yü but failed to capture him. He did, however, do justice to his campaign by cutting off nineteen thousand Hun heads. Ho, it is believed followed a more easterly course but was even more successful: he 'cut off heads and captured prisoners to the number of more than seventy thousand'. By this time virtually the whole of the Gobi Desert, much of present-day Inner and Outer Mongolia and the westerly province of Kansu,

132

Right : One of the principal motives in the expansion of the Chinese Empire during the Han Dynasty was the development of trade. Trains of camels, represented by this pottery model of the T'ang Dynasty, traversed the desert wastes laden with silks for the rich markets of the Near East and the Roman Empire were in Chinese hands. Commanderies were established in the newly acquired territories and Chinese people imported in order to retain control of the area and to develop whatever resources were available.

Emperor Wu also sought allies to assist him in his fight against the Hsiung-nu. To this end he declared his intention of finding the Yüeh-chih, a Central Asian people who it is thought were the easternmost extension of the Indo-European-speaking peoples. They had once occupied areas in western China, the modern province of Kansu, but had been driven out by the Hsiung-nu. From captured Hsiung-nu it appeared that the King of the Yüeh-chih had been defeated around 140 BC, and 'his skull had been made into a drinking vessel'. The Yüeh-chih fled westwards, far beyond the Tarim Basin to the Kushan territory of Afghanistan and Ferghana. To the military tactician Wu it seemed clear that with their co-operation in the west the Huns could be trapped in a pincer movement. As early as 139 BC, therefore, he dispatched an emissary, Chang Ch'ien, to seek out the Yüeh-chih and negotiate a pact with them against the Huns.

In order to reach their new lands Chang had to cross the Gobi Desert and the Tarim Basin, vast stretches of territory which were predominantly under

133

Hsiung-nu control. Almost inevitably, he was captured and taken before the Hun leader, the Shan-yü, who demanded: 'The Yüeh-chih people live to the north of me, what does the Han mean by trying to send an envoy to them? Do you suppose that if I tried to send an embassy to the kingdom of Yüeh in the south-east [of China] the Han would let my men pass through China?' The Hsiung-nu were clearly suspicious of an alliance between their two principal enemies and detained Chang Ch'ien and his embassy for over ten years. The Chinese envoy even took a Hun wife and became almost assimilated into their society.

But secretly Chang Ch'ien never betrayed his Imperial mission. As the restrictions on his movements relaxed he seized an opportunity to escape, and the embassy resumed its journey westward, and reached the kingdom of Ta-yüan (Ferghana), in present-day southern Russia to the east of the Caspian Sea. The King of Ta-yüan, who had heard of the great wealth and power of the Han and was delighted to receive Chang and his embassy, assisted them by providing guides to lead them to the Yüeh-chih. They travelled over the Pamir Mountains, through the kingdom of Transoxiana, and Chang, after nearly eleven years, eventually reached his destination and found the Yüeh-chih in Bactria.

Here in the rich fertile lands to the west of the Pamir Mountains and north of the Hindu Kush the Yüeh-chih had made their home. Having displaced the earlier Greek kingdoms, they had set about establishing themselves, and, protected by the mountains, were recuperating after years of harassment by the Hsiung-nu. Later they invaded parts of northern India and set up the Kushan Dynasty. To Chang Ch'ien's bitter disappointment, he found his potential allies a contented and flourishing people, whose king had no intention whatsoever of becoming needlessly involved with their former enemies.

Chang's description of his immense journey, the countries he saw and the new homeland of the Yüeh-chih, which he presented to the Emperor when he finally returned to Ch'ang-an in 126 BC, is glowing:

Ta-yüan [Ferghana] lies south-west of the territory of the Hsiung-nu, some ten thousand *li* [about 3,500 miles] directly west of China. The people are settled in the land ploughing the fields and growing rice and wheat. They also make wine out of grapes. The region has many fine horses which sweat blood; their forbears are supposed to have been foaled from heavenly horses. The people live in houses in

Right : Bronze chariot jingle of the Western Han Dynasty

fortified cities, there being some seventy or more cities of various sizes in the region. The population numbers several hundred thousand. The people fight with bows and spears and can shoot on horseback.

In An-hsi [Parthia] the people are settled on the land, cultivating the fields and growing rice and wheat. They have walled cities like the people of Ta-yüan, the region containing several hundred cities of various sizes. The kingdom, which borders the Kuei [Oxus] River, is very large, measuring several thousand *li* square. Some of the inhabitants are merchants who travel by carts or boats to neighbouring countries, sometimes journeying several thousand *li*. The coins of the country are made of silver and bear the face of the king. When the king dies, the currency is immediately changed and new coins issued with the face of the successor. The people keep records by writing horizontally on strips of leather.

T'iao-chih [Mesopotamia] is situated several thousand *li* west of An-hsi and borders the Western Sea [this was probably the Persian Gulf]. It is hot and damp, and the people live by cultivating the fields and planting rice. In this region live great birds which lay eggs as large as pots. The people are very numerous and are ruled by many petty chiefs. The ruler of An-hsi gives orders to these chiefs and regards them as his vassals. The people are very skilful at performing tricks that amaze the eye.

Chang's conclusions about his travels through the rich and fertile lands encouraged Emperor Wu and the Han Court to adopt even more ambitious plans. Wealthy the states of An-hsi, Ta-yüan and the others may have been, but Chang considered them militarily weak, and of course they had all heard of the great wealth and power of the Han. Although the Yüeh-chih were strong in arms they might perhaps be won over with tribute and then Wu could 'extend his domain ten thousand *li*, attract to his Court men of strange

A bronze spearhead dating from the
Western Han Dynasty

customs who would come translating and retranslating their languages, and his might would become known to all the lands within the four seas'. Thus the stage was set for a period of concerted expansion of the Chinese Empire.

Some years later, in 115 BC, Chang Ch'ien set off on yet another mission, this time to the kingdom of Wu-sun in the Ili Valley to the north of the Tarim Basin. Chang had heard of these people while living in captivity with the Hsiung-nu.

When I was living among the Hsiung-nu [he had reported], I heard about the king of the Wu-sun people, who is named K'un-mo. K'un-mo's father was the ruler of a small state on the western border of Hsiung-nu territory. The Hsiung-nu attacked and killed the father and K'un-mo, then only a baby, was cast out in the wilderness to die. But the birds came and flew over the place where he was, bearing meat in their beaks, and the wolves suckled him, so that he was able to survive. When the Shan-yü heard of this he was filled with wonder and, believing that K'un-mo was a God, he took him in and reared him. When K'un-mo had grown to manhood, the Shan-yü put him in command of a band of troops and he several times won merit in battle. The Shan-yü then made him the leader of the people whom his father had ruled in former times and ordered him to guard the western forts . . . soon he had twenty or thirty thousand skilled archers who were trained in aggressive warfare. When the Shan-yü died K'un-mo led his people far away, declared himself an independent ruler, and refused any longer to journey to the meetings of the Hsiung-nu Court.

K'un-mo's breakaway kingdom annoyed the Hsiung-nu intensely, but despite their repeated attacks, the kingdom of Wu-sun survived and flourished. The Huns finally decided that K'un-mo could indeed be a god and left him well alone. Nevertheless both Emperor Wu and Chang Ch'ien saw another potential ally in these people, and so he journeyed once more into the wastelands of Central Asia. Chang's embassy consisted of three hundred men, each supplied with two horses and in order to gain the favours of the Wu-sun they also took 'tens of thousands of cattle and sheep and carried gold and silk goods worth a hundred billion cash'.

But once again Chang failed to establish an alliance, for there were contending factions in Wu-sun and, in any event, none had yet heard of the wealth and power of Han China, so they could see no benefit in co-operation. The Chinese envoy did, however, manage to persuade some twenty representatives of the kingdom to return with him to Ch'ang-an, where they saw 'with their own eyes the breadth and greatness of the Han Empire!'

As a result China managed to establish formal relations with the Wu-sun, and also with the Yüeh-chih. This was an important step forward, for China thereby achieved a firm foothold in these Central Asian states with a view to future military undertakings, and was also able to watch over the developing trade-routes, along which precious cargoes of silk were exported westwards for the ladies of the Roman Empire.

It was not until after Chang Ch'ien's death that the Hsiung-nu learnt of the relations established between China and the kingdoms of the Wu-sun and the Yüeh-chih. With the threat of these alliances, and the Han constantly gaining territories and setting up provinces in the old Hun lands to the north of the Great Wall, the position of the whole Hsiung-nu state was threatened. The Chinese position was now sufficiently strong for them to feel that the Hsiung-nu could be forced to submit and acknowledge Chinese suzerainty. The outspoken envoy Yang Hsin was sent to the Shan-yü to discuss terms, but the Hun leader showed no liking for his uncompromising attitude. After imperiously refusing to present his credentials Yang announced to the Shan-yü: 'If you wish to conclude a peace alliance, you must send your heir to the Han Court as hostage.' The Hun King replied: 'That is not the way things were done under the old alliance. Under the old alliance the Han always sent us an Imperial princess, as well as allotments of silk, foodstuffs, and other goods, in order to secure peace, while we for our part refrained from making trouble on the border. Now you want to go against the old ways and make me send my son as hostage. I have no use for such proposals!' Nevertheless, negotiations continued: the highly sophisticated Court of Imperial China against the wily nomadic Hun King.

In 107 BC, Wang Wu was sent to discuss matters with the Huns, and once again the Shan-yü adopted a mild and conciliatory attitude; if he was to accede to them at least he wanted a fair share of the spoils. He even expressed a wish to travel to Ch'ang-an 'and visit the Son of Heaven so that face to face we may swear a pact by brotherhood'.

Emperor Wu took the Hun approach seriously and built a special palace in the capital to accommodate the Shan-yü. But once again all was in vain. An important emissary sent by the Hsiung-nu to Ch'ang-an unfortunately died shortly after his arrival in China. The Shan-yü, convinced that his envoy had been murdered, promptly withdrew from negotiations and recommenced his military adventures against the Middle Kingdom. Gradually the might of the massive Chinese armies pushed the Hsiung-nu further and further to the north-west. In 105 BC China invaded and took possession of Ta-yüan, or Ferghana, thus ensuring an ample supply of the famous horses 'which sweated blood' and which were so vital to their military campaigns.

138   The Chinese advancement continued relentlessly westwards towards the

Right: The massed cavalry of bronze horses and soldiers from the Eastern Han tomb at Leitai in Kansu province. It was from these areas of west China that many of the great military expeditions against the Huns commenced

Roman Empire after the death of the redoubtable Emperor Wu in 87 BC. Vast armies of Chinese soldiers, equipped with the strong Ferghana horses and new sophisticated crossbows, and supported by supplies from freshly established commanderies and kingdoms in the occupied lands, continued to harass the Hsiung-nu and push them further to the north and west. There was by now no question of Han Chinese militarism being motivated by considerations of defence. The continuing reports of new, rich and fertile lands to the west of the Central Asian deserts and the first tentative contacts with the easternmost of the Mediterannean peoples had opened new vistas for China. In addition, they now realised that they had both the ability and resources to conquer those 'twilight' kingdoms which acted as a buffer between the two giants, the Roman and the Chinese Empires.

In 42 BC, yet another Chinese army, this time some forty thousand strong, crossed the Pamir Mountains, passed through the newly Sinicised state of Ferghana and took the former Greek kingdom of Sodgiana, in what is now south-western Russia. Here the Chinese defeated some remnants of the Hsiung-nu, now principally inhabiting the steppe lands of south central Russia, and what was possibly a captive group of Roman soldiers. Chinese armies had extended the Han Empire across the desert wasteland and mountain ranges of Central Asia to within sight of the Roman Empire, over two thousand miles from their capital city at Ch'ang-an. This was a far greater distance than the Roman legions ever reached from Rome, and undertaken in the face of immensely difficult communications.

Emperor Wu had employed hundreds of thousands of cavalrymen and foot soldiers in the vast waves of armies he had flung at the Hsiung-nu. But still he searched for other means of defeating them. He conceived a plan of outflanking them from the east and to this end occupied the northern parts of Chosōn which, like its modern counterpart Korea, was then a semi-Sinicised state. At its capital, now the modern city of Pyongyong, capital city of North Korea, the Chinese established Lolang commandery, whose tombs have produced some of the finest examples of Han art, particularly lacquer.

Chosōn, although nominally independent, had long been under Chinese influence and to a certain extent the Han Emperor was able to dictate and influence her smaller neighbour. When King Wei Yu-ch'ü of Chosōn seemed to adopt an anti-Chinese policy, forcing many Han settlers to flee the country, the Emperor dispatched a senior official, She Ho, to rebuke the King and to warn him to mend his ways. She Ho was accompanied back to the border by the King's assistant, Chang, and when they arrived at the Pei River the Chinese envoy turned and stabbed the Korean to death. He then dashed across the river into Han China. Emperor Wu was pleased, but King Wei was infuriated by the treachery of the Chinese. Almost immediately a force of Korean troops crossed the border, and attacked and killed She Ho. Military conflict was inevitable. The Chinese campaign was conducted by two generals who became irreconcilable in their approach, and Emperor Wu had to intervene. In retrospect the whole Korean campaign was a needless disaster; the squabbles between the Chinese generals resulted in an unnecessarily protracted campaign – as Ssu-ma Ch'ien records, 'both armies disgraced themselves and none of their leaders were enfeoffed as marquises'; moreover the eastern outflanking movement against the Hsiung-nu never proved a practical proposition.

There is no doubt that Emperor Wu was infected with the 'Alexander complex', the desire to conquer and expand the Empire as far as practical military considerations would allow, and often beyond those limits. We have seen how he looked to the north, west and east, but he also looked to the south for more lands to conquer. By comparison with the difficulties he encountered in Central Asia, the already semi-Sinicised states of the south presented no problem. In 111 BC, the Han conquered the state of southern Yüeh (Nan-yüeh) occupying the modern provinces of Kwangtung, Kwangsi and parts of North Vietnam, with the capital in the vicinity of Canton. From here the

141

Bronze horse and chariot from the Eastern Han tombs at Leitai in Kansu province

Han troops moved westwards again and took parts of the modern provinces of Kweichou and Yunnan, across to the borders of Burma.

The pure desire for territorial gains was not the only motive behind the Han Chinese drives in these directions. Their occupation of the southerly coastline provided them with fresh outlets for their seaborne trade to India and the West. Emperor Wu may also have seen opportunities of further territorial gains in south-east Asia and the Philippines. Even though under independent rule, these regions were becoming increasingly influenced by their mighty neighbour.

The area of south-western China which the Han occupied during the reign of Emperor Wu was previously ruled over by a number of independent chiefs. These 'south-western barbarian' tribal chiefs wore 'their hair in mallet-shaped fashion, work the fields, and live in settlements. Beyond them to the west, in the region from T'ung-shih east to Yeh-yü are the tribes called Sui and K'un-ming, whose people all braid their hair and move from place to place with their herds of domestic animals, having no fixed homes and no chieftains.' These fragmented communities were no match for the Son of Heaven's well-organised soldiers and the Chinese histories merely record that they were invaded and occupied. There seems to have been no significant battles fought, no opposition met. Here again the Chinese saw potential trade-routes, through the forests and mountains of modern Burma, to India and thence to the West. Unlike the seaborne trade from the ports of the southern coast, this difficult overland route never fulfilled Wu's hopes.

It was inevitable that after the death of Emperor Wu the momentum of Han expansion should be lost. The campaigns in the south and the west, motivated not by the needs of defence but purely by ambition, were never followed up by later rulers of the Dynasty. But in the west there were two factors to be considered. First, there remained the problem of the Hsiung-nu, who in spite of being removed far from the Great Wall, were still a threat to the more distant outposts of the Chinese Empire. Second, the trade-routes to the West had to be protected and developed. It was, therefore, a matter of maintaining the *status quo*, of protecting territories gained rather than of seeking more acquisitions.

Han China was soon to be thrown into the turmoil of Wang Mang's usurpation of the Imperial throne. During these turbulent years the Han armies were in some disarray and many were recalled to attend to domestic uprisings. Some territory in Central Asia was lost and it was not until the throne had been firmly re-established with the Han line and stability had returned to the Middle Kingdom later in the first century AD, that China was able again to look to her western borders.

By 80 AD the whole of the Tarim Basin was firmly under Chinese rule and soon after Pan Ch'ao, brother of the famous Han historian Pan Ku, was leading massive Chinese armies over the Pamir Mountains and conquering the whole area as far as the Caspian Sea. The Kushan Empire of the Yüeh-chih to the south was also taken.

Pan Ch'ao himself remained in Central Asia; perhaps he sensed the great wealth and culture that lay beyond the westernmost extension of the Empire. In between the two great civilisations of Rome and China lay Persia, ruled at the time by the Parthians. They must have felt like a nut in a pair of nut-crackers, as the Romans in the west and the Chinese in the east advanced remorselessly. The eager Pan Ch'ao in 97 AD sent an envoy, Kan Ying, to go to Persia and thence to travel to Rome, known then to the Chinese as Ta-ch'in. Having first arrived in Persia Kan was persuaded by the Parthians not to continue his journey to Rome and thus the fascinating possibility of a Roman-Chinese alliance was lost. He did, however, reach the eastern parts of Mesopotamia (T'iao-chih) and the head of the Persian Gulf, and his reports no doubt infused Pan with still more ambition.

However, circumstances were by now beginning to turn against the Chinese. The Later (or Eastern) Han Dynasty, never somehow achieved the vitality of its predecessor. The later emperors were but pale reflections of the mighty Kao Tsu or Wu, and only Pan Ch'ao among the generals could be considered the equal of Wei Ch'ing or Ho Ch'ü-ping. No doubt the Imperial Treasury was beginning to feel the strain of maintaining vast armies over two thousand miles from the capital. The cost of supporting both them and the enormous complex of supply-lines across the Central Asian wastes must have been immense, and the Imperial Court was becoming more and more disinclined to support such seemingly unrewarding expenditure.

In many ways the success of China in Central Asia in the first century AD was the achievement of one man, Pan Ch'ao. After Pan Ch'ao's death in 102 AD there was a gradual retreat. The great era of Chinese expansion had reached its limit, and never again was an Emperor of the Middle Kingdom to rule over such a vast and far-flung Empire.

Above all, these three centuries of exciting, vigorous and adventurous rule had opened new vistas for China, which up till then had always been an inward-looking country. The Chinese had been forced to recognise the existence of other peoples, other cultures and other civilisations. We shall see how the Han Court was influenced by Western and Near Eastern ideals, but in general China was reluctant to accept outside ideas and influences.

One important exception was the introduction of the Buddhist faith, which occurred early in the Later (or Eastern) Han period. Contact with north Indian civilisation was made possible by the expansion of the Han westwards through Central Asia, and by the journeys of Chang Ch'ien. Indeed, it has often been suggested that Chang returned to the Middle Kingdom with information about the Buddha. In the spring of 121 BC, the General Ho Ch'ü-ping led a troop of ten thousand cavalrymen more than one thousand *li* beyond Mount Yen-chih and attacked the Hsiung-nu. After killing or capturing over eighteen thousand of the enemy and defeating the king of the Hsiu-t'u – whose kingdom was situated in the western part of Hsiung-nu territory – he seized the 'golden man which he used in worshipping heaven'. Was this perhaps an image of the Buddha?

The most popular story among the myths and legends concerning the introduction of Buddhism to China is the 'Dream of Emperor Ming', who ruled from 58 to 75 AD. One night, he dreamt of a golden deity flying in front of his palace. The following day he recounted to his ministers the details of his dream and one of them, Fu Yi, replied that he had heard of a sage in India who had achieved salvation and that he was called the Buddha. Although one is bound to ask how and where Fu Yi obtained this information the Emperor found the explanation sufficiently convincing and ordered a deputation to go in search of this mysterious foreign deity. There is no consistency in the facts concerning the mission, the dates of both the departure and the return vary, and one account even suggests that Chang Ch'ien himself, who lived some two centuries previously, led the mission!

However unreliable the story of the Emperor's dream may be, it appears certain that the Buddhist faith had gained a foothold in China by the end of the first century AD. Descriptions of the Eastern Han capital at Loyang refer to Buddhist temples and communities of monks within the city walls. At that time there was also a growing community of Central Asian origin, principally merchants and traders living in the Chinese capital, who no doubt were familiar with the religion of their homeland. The endless caravans carrying silks to the markets of the Near East and Rome must have returned to China with stories of the faith, for Central Asia was dotted with Buddhist communities which frequently offered food and shelter to merchants during the course of their long and arduous journey. However, the inherent resistance to foreign ideals and cultures was a formidable barrier to the acceptance and development of the religion in China. Confucianism and Taoism were fundamental to Han society and seemed to fulfil all the needs of the people. That Buddhism finally overcame those obstacles is testimony to the strength and imagination of the faith and to the far-reaching effects of the expansion and development of China during the Han Dynasty.

Right : A bronze lion, probably part of the support for a vessel, in the style of the Late Chou–Early Han inlaid bronze tradition. This is a later copy dating from the Sung Dynasty.
Over top left : Gilt-bronze bridle cheek-piece. Late Chou Dynasty, fourth–third centuries BC
Over bottom left : Chariot fitting in the form of a bull's head, inlaid with gold. Late Chou Dynasty, fifth–fourth centuries BC

8 ART AND CULTURE: the Age of Realism

WE SEE THE CONSEQUENCES OF THE EVENTS DESCRIBED IN THE previous chapter most clearly expressed in the art of the Han period. The expansion of the Empire to territories and cultures previously totally unknown to China stimulated the imagination of a nation already brimming with strength and confidence.

Pre-Han art was dominated by the culture of one of the most sophisticated and technically superior Bronze Ages the world has ever known. But by the fifth or fourth centuries BC, after a period of over one thousand years, the bronze tradition in China was losing its impetus, originality and vitality. The dynamic and often extrovert forms of the Shang and Early Chou ritual vessels gave way to derivative types in which the emphasis was placed on surface decorative patterns. Although based on the décor and designs of the early bronzes these later interpretations gradually evolved into complex interlaced patterns that were far removed from the originals.

Shortly before the Han Dynasty was established, new inspiration was found and the patterns were released from the tense abstractions of monster masks that so dominated the bronze designs of the Shang and Early Chou. In their place there came a dual expression, of delicate but strictly geometric designs, and a more exuberant expression of semi-naturalistic forms generally based on the dragon in bold sweeping spirals. Both styles were fully exploited in the beautiful inlaid bronze vessels and fittings and the painted pottery vessels of the Warring States period (481–221 BC). These are typical of the fine and often complex decorative patterns which characterise the art of the immediate pre-Han era, and illustrate how the ornament and décor no longer formed an integral part of the vessel, as was the case with Shang and Early Chou bronzes. And yet there still existed a precise relationship between form and decoration. The bias had now changed so that surface decoration was the dominant feature, but the manner in which these patterns enveloped and expressed the form is indicative of a highly sophisticated and technically supreme art form.

As a result of the prodigious expansion of the Chinese Empire during the Han period there was a tremendous influx of new ideas and artistic styles. Naturalistic representation was used in early Near Eastern and Central Asian art under the influence of ancient Greece and Rome, but it had never been a feature of ancient Chinese art. It was these Mediterranean styles as interpreted and modified by the peoples of Central Asia which provided

146

much of the initial inspiration for Han art. Not that the art of Han China became in any way derivative, this was never a feature of Chinese art. In later eras, for example during the T'ang Dynasty (618–906 AD), foreign ideas and styles were integrated into the native art, but then again the foreign styles were assimilated, adapted and Sinicised so that, as with the Han, the art styles were always characteristically Chinese.

One of the principal vehicles for the transmission of Western styles to Han China was their old enemy, the Hsiung-nu. The art of the steppes and the Ordos region was inspired by the environment, but stylistically influenced by Greek and Roman ideals. Typical of Hsiung-nu art are openwork bronze plaques, probably harness-fittings, decorated with confronting horses. The subject-matter reflects the importance of the horse in Hun society, but the confronting composition and the semi-naturalistic openwork surround are clearly Western-inspired.

Another consequence of the Han occupation of areas well outside the original boundaries of China is that Han art has been found not only in China proper, but also in southern Russia, Mongolia and Central Asia. The famous expeditions of the Russian archaeologist Kozlov in northern Mongolia in

1924–5 retrieved examples of classic Han art, particularly textiles, as well as objects representative of the native Hsiung-nu. Sir Aurel Stein in his expeditions to Khotan and other areas of Central Asia in 1913–16 recovered both characteristic Central Asian art, and silks from metropolitan China. These finds illustrate how Chinese culture and influence spread along with trade at the time, for the preponderance of silks suggest a sizeable commerce in that material along the famous 'silk road'.

Another aspect of Han society also radically affected artistic style. In the feudal period of the pre-Han, art was produced solely in the service of ritual and ceremony for the Imperial family and the feudal nobility. In the Han period, art ceased to be the prerogative of such a minority, for the growing wealth of the country as a whole and the newly emergent classes of officials and merchants produced a wider circle of patrons whose requirements were not dominated by ancient ritual and ceremonial. Their motives were the sheer indulgence of having beautiful objects with which to adorn their homes and palaces and to increase their stature in the face of the common people.

Some of the finest extant works of Han art have come from tombs far away from the capital cities of Ch'ang-an and Loyang. Man-ch'eng, for example, is some five hundred miles from the sites of the Han capitals, while other notable Han sites at Lolang in Korea and Ch'ang-sha in Hunan are even further away. Nowhere is the fresh naturalistic approach of the Han better expressed than in the engraved stone reliefs which formed part of the structure of these tombs. Immensely valuable as documents detailing daily secular and religious life in early China, they are also among the most beautiful examples of early pictorial art.

A small stone shrine marks the tomb of a certain Han general, Chu Wei, who died in 50 AD on the outskirts of the small town of Chin-hsiang in Shantung province. Beneath is the vaulted brick tomb itself, the chambers lined with engraved stone slabs depicting courtly scenes of audiences and banquets. The artist has employed that characteristically unsettling Chinese perspective, producing a rhythmic order in the disposition of the figures all bedecked in their full flowing robes. Unlike the funerary objects, bronze vessels, pottery urns and figures which assisted the dead man in the hereafter, these secular pictures were intended to recall and commemorate occasions of honour and glory during his life, as well as his favourite pastimes and pleasures.

148

Detail of a small bronze belt-hook inlaid with gold and turquoise. Late Chou Dynasty, fourth–third centuries BC

Even more comprehensive are the stone engravings from the tomb of the Wu family at Chia-hsing, also in Shantung province. An inscription records the building of these now famous tombs: 'In the first year of *Chien-ho* [147 AD] the cyclical year *ting-hai*, in the third month which began with the day *Keng-hsu* on the fourth day *Kuei-ch'ou* the filial sons Wu Shih-kung and his younger brothers Sui-tsung, Ching-lsing and K'ai-ming, erected these pillars, made by the sculptor Li Ti-mao, styled Meng-fu, at a cost of 150,000 pieces of money. Su Tsung made a pair of stone lions which cost 40,000 cash [originally a pair of stone lions marked the entrance of the tomb].'

There are two unusual features in this inscription which indicate the changing values and traditions during the Han Dynasty. First, the sculptor is named. With the exception of painters Chinese craftsmen and artists have always tended to remain anonymous. Second, the rather vulgar mention of the cost would seem to indicate that with the advent of a wealthy society so there came an increased respect for that wealth.

The techniques employed in the carving of these engravings is as distinctive as their style. The background was cut away, leaving the actual design in relief, which was then engraved with the detail. The background was scraped with vertical striations to provide a vivid texture to contrast with the flat smooth surface of the relief design. Here once again secular scenes from the lives of the deceased dominate the compositions. These reliefs also illustrate other characteristics of Han pictorial art; the flat, two-dimensional schematisation, the lack of spatial depth and the absence of a consistent base or ground line. Some of the Wu family reliefs do display an attempt to represent depth – for example, the chariots and carriages are shown in three-quarter view, as are the horses pulling the vehicle – but with the flat profile and silhouetted human figures the sense of depth is at the best only very tentatively suggested.

The manner and style of these reliefs emphasise the fundamental characteristic of Han art; the domination of surface ornament and design over form. We see basically similar designs of figures, Court and hunting scenes, battles, and mythological or ceremonial events applied to bronze vessels of the Early Han, and used in the same way as patterns to fit a surface area. As such they, too, were inevitably subject to formalisation as the balanced compositions of the Wu family tomb reliefs show.

150   Many Han tombs were lined with stamped or moulded pottery tiles and

Right: Detail of the reverse side of a bronze mirror showing scrolling dragons against a spiralled background. Late Chou Dynasty, fourth century BC

bricks, which, although using the same basic artistic style, express a freer, less formal approach. Undoubtedly medium and technique were vital considerations in this distinction. In these tiles the horsemen, chariots and carriages give a much more vivid sense of reality and movement and contrast with the often icy stiffness of the stone engravings.

The Han pictorial stone engravings or impressed pottery tiles have no counterpart in earlier Chinese art. They must, therefore, be considered as imports from the Roman and Hellenistic influenced areas of Central Asia. There are obvious resemblances between these reliefs and those of Assyria, Greece and Rome. However, it is important to appreciate that it was the concept that was imported, and subsequently adapted, for the style and the manner of the execution is entirely Chinese. These strictly formal two-dimensional representations have no accurate Western counterpart.

The more relaxed and fluent style of the pottery reliefs associates them with painted designs. Again we must look to the tomb interiors, for it is only here that examples of Han painting have been preserved in any quantity. And once again we see how medium and technique influence artistic style, for there is a fluency and flexibility in the use of the brush which permits subtle inflexions of line and colour that immediately give effect to depth and volume.

The overall compositions of the painted tomb walls differ little from those in stone or pottery, as indeed do the subjects depicted or the sense of formalisation to the compositions as a whole. These are basic characteristics of Han art. But in the paintings the noble courtiers and officials acquire a reality and a certain dignity as they seem to glide along the tomb walls. Equally, the ability to express and to adapt detail features permits greater scope in the portrayal of attitudes and mannerisms, as illustrated by figures from the tomb at Wang-tu in Hopei province, which are often distinctly amusing.

The same comparisons may be made with paintings of horses and carriages and their stone relief counterparts. The procession of carriages painted along the wall of a tomb at Hou-yin-shan in Shantung province has a lightness of touch that is both gay and amusing. However, there is still no attempt to imply depth realistically, whereas those in a tomb at Pei-yüan in Liaoning show the three-quarter view so characteristic of the stone engraving. In these paintings yet another feature of Han pictorial art is vividly expressed, the leaping or galloping horse, also inspired by the naturalism of contemporary Western and Near Eastern art and subsequently given full and lively expression by the Chinese.

The horse, and in particular those imported for use in the Han cavalry from Central Asia, which included the famous Ferghana horse, played an increasingly important role in the life of the Chinese people. The horses that 'sweated blood' were evidently a cut above the rugged Mongolian ponies which were in common use in China, especially in the north. Nowhere is the respect for the noble Ferghana horse more graphically expressed than in the recently discovered bronze models from Wu Wei county in Kansu province. The location of the discovery of these truly magnificent bronzes is significant, for Kansu is in the far west of China, on the borders of Central Asia, starting point for so many of the military campaigns against the Hsiung-nu. All the strength and sturdiness of the animals is dramatically expressed in these most lively and vivacious works, and yet the head and features are modelled with a sensitivity and naturalism that is uncharacteristic of the earliest Chinese art, but so indicative of the new Han approach. The most outstanding is the now famous 'flying horse'. With its head and tail held proudly high, and just one hoof touching the ground, it gives a vivid and tremendous impression of speed and enduring strength. This and other horses were among a cache of bronzes, which included horses and carriages, horses and

152

Top right : Gilt bronze plaque, possibly from a chariot or harness, showing two fighting horses. Hsiung-nu art from the Ordos regions. Third century BC
Bottom right : A reconstruction of a stone relief from the offertory shrines at the graves of the Wu family, wealthy members of the official classes, in the Eastern Han Dynasty. The formalised but dramatic scheme is heightened by the silhouette style of these stone relief pictures

153

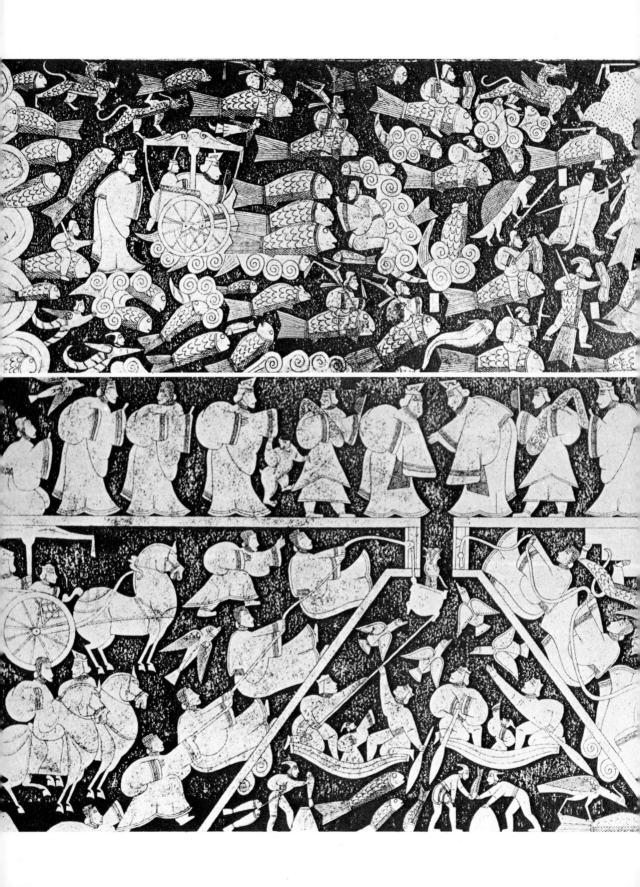

riders, as well as lacquer-ware, jades and gold pieces, discovered in 1969.

The companion horses and carriages are three-dimensional models of the painted and engraved examples we have already encountered. Here again there is a strength and nobility in the modelling of the horses, the four legs held tensely as if straining to be unleashed, contrasting strongly with the official sitting serenely in his canopied carriage. Here the dynamic Han naturalism finds unique and complete fulfilment.

Painted lacquers form another category of pictorial art in which we see the influence and adaptation of Western ideals. From the Lolang commandery in present-day Korea – another acquisition due to the expansion of the Empire – have come a quantity of painted lacquers. The well-known 'painted basket' excavated from the tomb of a minor local official is decorated with traditional Confucian and historical figures, famous rulers and paragons of filial piety, all drawn with freedom and animation. There is also a successful attempt to establish a dialogue between the figures, employing natural gestures and poses. Although set on a base line, 'breathing and living' space and depth is implied by the varying profile, full-face and three-quarter views of the figures, and by the natural and fluent fall of the robes across the shoulders and onto the floor. Like their stone silhouette relief and painted tomb wall counterparts, there is no attempt to provide a setting for these figures and yet they achieve a convincing naturalism through lively juxtaposition and animated communication. Many of the Han lacquers from Lolang bear inscriptions giving the dates of manufacture, varying between 85 BC and 71 AD, and stating that they were made in far-off Szechwan province in western China where the Han Imperial lacquer workshops were situated.

The peculiar qualities of lacquer which render it virtually indestructible under certain conditions – above all in waterlogged burials – have resulted in some amazing finds. In 1972 the body of the consort of the Marquis Li Tsang was unearthed near the city of Ch'ang-sha in Hunan province in a remarkable state of preservation. The corpse itself was intact, having been wrapped in layers of woven and embroidered silks and then set inside a lacquered wood coffin, painted with dragon- and cloud-inspired scrolling motifs. The soft damp soil of this region of China made it impossible to hollow out a mausoleum like that at Man-ch'eng, and instead the coffin was placed in a pit, some seventy feet deep, lined with a series – six in all – of lacquer-painted wood sections. Inside the cavities between the linings were preserved over one 155

Reconstruction of a stone relief picture from the Wu family shrines in Shantung province, illustrating in the same 'silhouette' style the story of the 'attempted recovery of the Chou cauldron'

thousand burial objects; an array of beautiful and perfectly preserved lacquered boxes and dishes, wine cups and jars, wood and bamboo utensils, silk brocades, gauzes and embroideries, pottery vessels, serried ranks of small wooden images, musical instruments, and a stunning silk banner. This last was painted with mythological scenes of 'Shen I shooting down the Nine Suns' and of 'Lady Ch'ang O flies to the moon'. Shen I, who lived in the middle of the third millennium BC, was an archer of great renown. Named 'Divine Archer' by the Emperor Yao, he was responsible for dispelling the Nine False Suns. Lady Ch'ang stole from her husband the drug of immortality, which had been given to him by Hsi Wang-mu, the Queen Mother of the West, and fled to safety on the moon. Below are painted scenes from the daily life of the mistress of the household, including a feast, such as those we have encountered on stone tomb engravings. Even caskets and boxes of food; rice, vegetables, pickles, pears and melons, have survived the two thousand one hundred years underground, without total decay.

Unlike the later (first and second centuries AD) figure-ornamented lacquers from Korea, these Ch'ang-sha examples are painted with vibrant scrolling patterns characteristic of inlaid bronzes. Indeed, the shapes of many of the

A reconstructed painting of a carriage procession based on a stone coffin painting discovered in 1953 at Hou-yin-shan in Shantung province. The inscription names the dead man as 'Lord Ch'un-yu'. Eastern Han Dynasty

Right: Detail of a tomb wall painting, illustrating officials. From a tomb at Wang-tu in Hopei province. Eastern Han Dynasty

vessels themselves, for example the square *hu*, were clearly inspired by bronze prototypes.

The dependence of Early Han lacquer art on the later Warring States bronze tradition is shared by the painted pottery vessels of the period. As the Bronze Age petered out, so it became necessary to find a substitute material, especially for tomb and burial objects. Ever since the beginning of the Shang Dynasty, *circa* 1500 BC, ceramic art had been somewhat overshadowed by the more sophisticated and impressive bronzes. But during the Warring States period fresh influences and the development of complex surface patterns provided new impetus for the ceramic industry. Many sites in China have turned up unglazed earthenware vessels painted in once bright colours; reds, blues, greens and ochres, with the swirling dragon designs or formalised geometric patterns of inlaid bronze vessels.

As the tendency towards naturalistic design gathered momentum in the Early Han and the opportunities for painting such décor on pottery vessels increased, so the ceramic industry gradually gained an ascendency over the bronze tradition. Many Early Han pottery urns are decorated with scenes of traditional mythology, or lively dragons and birds (principally the phoenix),

Detail of a tomb wall painting showing horses and carriages, executed in a lively and expressive manner, a feature of much Han representational art. From a tomb at Pei-yuan in Liaoning. Eastern Han Dynasty

Right: Pottery tomb model of a horse's head; its features show this to be one of the Central Asian breeds which were used so much in the military conflicts between the Chinese and the Hsiung-nu. Late Han Dynasty, third century AD

human figures and animals.

In the Later Han period the ceramic industry achieved further advancement with the development of high-fired wares; stonewares with feldspathic glazes. It was with this significant step forward that we see a certain individualism creeping back into the ceramic form. These wares were generally fired at a temperature around 1000 °C, much higher than the 700–800 °C required to fire the earlier earthenwares. The stoneware vessels were generally covered, on the upper part of the body, with an olive-green glaze which blended with the warm brown of the fired but unglazed lower part. Beneath the glaze were lightly engraved abstracted motifs, birds and dragons, often combined with a distinctive 'combed' wave pattern.

Earthenwares were still produced in large quantities, especially for burial objects. The range and variety of Han tomb figurines have provided us with much information about Han life and society. The models of courtiers, officials, servants, animals and buildings provide a unique picture of China some two thousand years ago. Among the most valuable are the models of houses and watchtowers, often multi-storeyed, with figures peering from behind pillars or leaning over balconies. Others represent miniature sheep-pens, with sheep and shepherd in attendance, or the popular models of stoves with utensils and food moulded on the top surface. These were generally covered with a green lead glaze, which acquires a silvery iridescence after long burial.

Unglazed painted funerary objects were also made, but it was a technique in general preserved for human figures. Typical are the impressively simple and serene standing figures of ladies, their hands held together and concealed beneath the voluminous sleeves of their robes. The simple but classic composition is emphasised by the flare of the robes at the hem, which always totally conceals the feet. Among the most unusual and amusing tomb figures ever found are the painted compositions unearthed in 1969 near the city of Chinan in Shantung province. Two groups of standing courtiers and officials look on while the tumblers perform their acrobatic feats. A group of accompanying musicians includes a drummer, a cymbalist and a percussionist on the stone chimes.

Another vitally important aspect of Han art was the silk industry. We have already seen evidence of a highly developed industry in China in the finds along the ancient silk roads through Central Asia. Sericulture in China goes

Right : The famous 'flying horse' from the hoard of bronze horses, chariots and riders, lacquerware, gold, and jade pieces discovered in 1969 in a tomb at Leitai, Wu-wei county, in Kansu province. Eastern Han Dynasty

Over : Bronze horses from the tomb at Leitai, reminders of the Han cavalry which campaigned constantly in Central Asia during the Han Dynasty

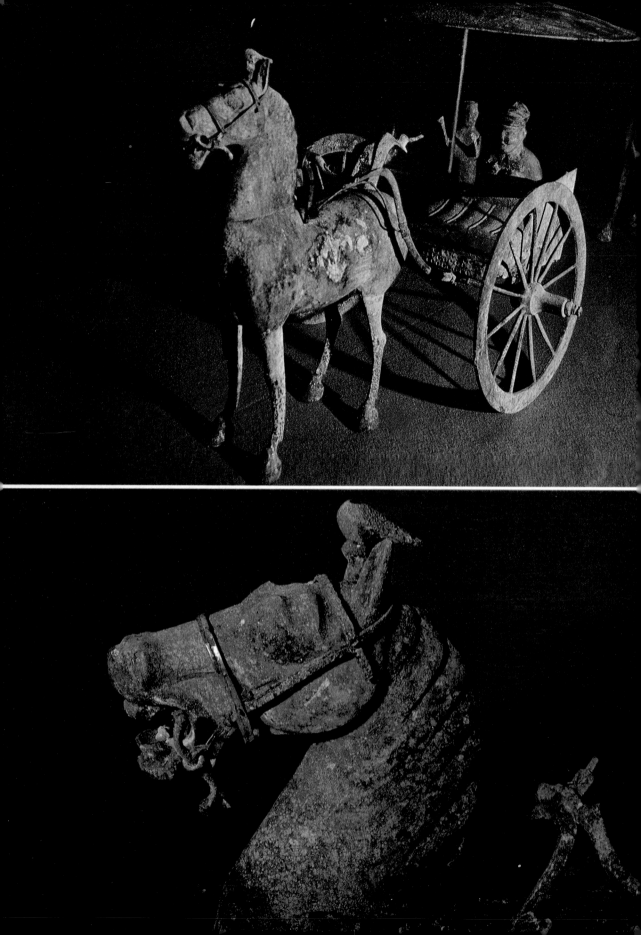

back at least as far as the Shang Dynasty, for excavated fragments of bronze vessels show traces of having been wrapped in silk. But it was not until the Han that the industry, on the evidence of surviving material, was fully exploited and established, and we cannot overlook the importance of contacts with the West in connection with these developments.

Han textile designs display all the elements of imaginative resources and catholicity of subject-matter that we have come to expect from a culture owing something to traditional Chinese ideas and something to newly imported Western concepts. The industry was undoubtedly stimulated by the ever-increasing demand for fine silks from far beyond the borders of China, especially the wealthy and expansive Mediterranean civilisations of Greece and Rome. Silk manufacture has always occupied a high place among China's industries and like lacquer, received Imperial patronage under the Han. State-owned factories were set up, principally in the eastern provinces – where the production of silk remains to this day one of the most important industries – to supply the Imperial Court and those of the enfeoffed kings and nobles with endless bolts of fine woven and embroidered silks for robes, ceremonial paraphernalia and hangings to ornament their palaces.

Although nothing remains of the actual machinery used for the silk-weaving, engraved stone reliefs have once again recorded details that would otherwise have been lost. On the evidence of these and from the nature of surviving fragments of woven material it would seem that the Han weavers used a type of draw-loom in which the warp threads were stretched horizontally along the length of the loom. The wefts were then inserted from side to side. These were not necessarily evenly inserted, for it is a characteristic of Han woven silks that they are warp patterned, unlike the weft-patterned Western types. Both the stone reliefs and the silk products themselves suggest that Chinese sericulture in the Han period was far in advance, by some six or seven centuries, of the industry in the West.

The mechanical nature of weaving implies a certain formalisation and repetition in the design; both qualities which we have seen to be characteristic of Han art. We find two basic types of design; one with a geometric basis, and one with a fluent spiralling or scrolling bias. The former group of designs relies heavily on the motifs of earlier bronzes; diaper patterns, lozenge-shaped designs and zig-zag bands. The second and more naturalistic group comprises designs of cloud-like scrolls, dragons, birds and landscape-inspired   161

Top left : An official's carriage : bronze
tomb figures from the Leitai tomb.
Eastern Han Dynasty
Bottom left : Bronze horse and
cavalryman from the Leitai tomb.
Eastern Han Dynasty

h may have their origin in the animal or cloud-inspired patterns.
...umes the two were combined and thus we find paired and confronting
birds and animals, a concept inspired by Western ideas, as we have seen in
the Hsiung-nu bronze plaques, set within lozenge patterns.

Although the bronze industry was being run down even before the advent
of the Han, it was by no means a spent force. The tombs of Prince Liu Sheng
and Princess Tou Wan have produced sufficient bronzes, of all types and of
high quality, to suggest a still-thriving industry. But it was, by comparison
with the Shang and Chou periods, a contracting industry. The immense
quantity and variety of impressive ritual vessels were no longer required, and
thus we find bronze being put to use for purely secular purposes. As such, they
lost much of their unique symbolism and inspired ornament – in fact many
Han bronzes are undecorated or only very sparsely so. Thus we find utilitarian
vessels now made of bronze; bowls like those from the Man-ch'eng tombs,
tripod cooking vessels with handles elegantly shaped in the form of a bird's
head and neck, ewers for heating and containing wine, and of course a wide
variety of food-containers.

Bronze mirrors form a substantial category in the repertoire of the Han

162

*Above : The painted lacquer coffin of
the consort of the Marquis Li Tsang*

*Right : The tomb at Mawangtui, near
Ch'ang-sha in Hunan, of the wife of
the Marquis of Ta (the Marquis Li
Tsang), showing the compartments
holding the various accessories, con-
tainers and food, around the coffin*

bronzesmith. The reverse side of the smooth, slightly convex and highly polished reflective surface, formed an ideal vehicle for the expression of all manner of religious and mythological notions. The earliest examples, dating back to the Warring States and Early Han periods (there is a small number of Chou examples), employ designs of scrolling dragons interlaced with lozenge forms, or with tightly interwoven patterns, related to both earlier bronze designs and contemporary, i.e. Han, lacquer and textile decorations. By the time of the Emperor Wu, however, his firm beliefs and interest in the Taoist religion inspired the bronze-casters to employ a wide variety of mythological and religious subjects as mirror décor. These included the Animals of the Four Quarters – the red bird of the south, the white tiger of the west, the azure dragon of the east and the black warrior (a tortoise) of the north, Hsi Wang-mu, the Queen Mother of the West – a very popular Taoist deity, and the TLV pattern which symbolised in all probability the relationship between heaven and earth. In Chinese cosmological symbolism the square represents the earth, and the circle the heavens.

As the need grew for more and more industrial and semi-industrial goods, especially agricultural implements and textile machinery, and the bronze

Above left : A square-shaped lacquer wine vessel, hu, from the Mawangtui tomb, illustrating the remarkable state of preservation
Above right : A lacquer tray with cups and bowls from the same burial

Right : Painted silk banner depicting 'Shen I shooting down the Nine Suns' and 'Lady Ch'ang O flies to the Moon' Over : Small wooden figures from the Mawangtui tomb, painted in imitation of the woven and embroidered silk robes

165

industry diminished, so the iron industry developed. Early in the Christian era there were as many as forty-eight government iron agencies, all in north China. It has been estimated that by the end of the first century AD, there were as many as one hundred thousand men employed in the iron- and copper-mines, these also owned and managed by the state.

Farming tools were the principal products, in particular, ploughshares and hoes, but few have survived, as such mundane and utilitarian objects were not considered worthy of a place in the tombs. Iron was also used for weapons, spears and arrow-heads as well as personal armour and helmets. Some idea of the volume of the industry may be obtained from the fact that soldiers were often provided with as many as one hundred and fifty iron arrow-heads when leaving for battle.

The Han was also a period of great literary activity. There was no lengthy and involved philosophical discussion on the scale of the preceding era – the Han people were too realistic, busy and practical – but much work was done in the field of collating and classifying earlier works, including those of the great philosophers of the Confucian and immediately post-Confucian periods. In addition there was both concern for and interest in the history of China, no

Above : Gilt-bronze belt-hook composed of a dragon and a tiger. Late Chou Dynasty, fourth–third centuries BC
Above right : Bronze plaque composed of bovine heads, representative of peri- *pheral Han art, from Shih-chai-shan in Yunnan province*
Right : Detail of the reverse side of a bronze mirror depicting the story of the loyal minister Wu Tzu-hsu. Eastern Han Dynasty

doubt inspired by the social revolutions which preceded the founding of the Dynasty. The first of China's standard histories, the *Records* (*Shih Chi*) of the Grand Historian of China, Ssu-ma Ch'ien, was written at the time of Emperor Wu. The author died in 90 BC.

Perhaps we may also associate with Han naturalism the increasing interest in and awareness of nature. The Han age produced many lyrical poems descriptive of both the beauty of nature and the depth of human emotions.

Broad flow the waters of the Yüan and the Hsiang;
Their two streams roar on to the Yangtze,
Long is the road and hidden in shadow;
The way I go is vast and far,
I sing to myself of my constant sorrow,
Lost in lamentation.
In the world no one knows me;
There is none to tell my heart to.
I must embrace my thoughts, hold fast my worth;
I am alone and without a mate.
Po Lo, judge of fine steeds, has long passed away;
Who now can tell the worth of a thoroughbred?

Man at his birth receives his fate,
And by it each life must be disposed.
I will calm my heart and pluck up my will;
What more have I to fear?
I know that death cannot be refused;
May I love life no longer!
This I proclaim to all worthy men:
I will be an example for you!

This somewhat melancholy poem by Ch'ü Yüan none the less reflects an attitude current during the Han period, the acceptance and recognition of destiny, and the notion that nature was a self-perpetuating force and man merely a part of it.

The advance in sciences and technology are among the greatest achievements of the Han period, and many treatises were written on the nature of the world, the heavens and earth, mathematics, medicine and warfare. Just as in the arts, this was a period of breaking new ground, of trial and experiment. There is even an attempt at aviation! In 19 AD, during the period of Wang Mang's usurpation, the Hsiung-nu were still a threat to the Empire and Wang was continually soliciting those of unique or extraordinary skill to find some way of conquering the Hun. An entry in the *Han Shu* for that year reads: 'One said that he was able to fly a thousand *li* in a day so that he could spy out the Huns. Wang Mang immediately had him try out his invention. He took the quills of a large bird to make his two wings; on both his head and his body he stuck feathers. He connected them by pivots. He flew several hundred double-paces and then he fell!'

There was still a curious ambivalence in the official doctrine of the Han emperors and their courts. On the one hand they practised the Confucian doctrine of order and discipline and on the other fervently believed in those unseen powers which were the forces behind nature and the universe. Thus a disastrous earthquake or drought was seen as a heavenly device to warn the Emperor that his shortcomings were being noticed. Such divergent attitudes were the source of much controversy and many writers and philosophers discussed and wrote at length on the relative merits of the supernatural viewpoint and the more logical and ordered Confucian viewpoint. In many ways the latter was more representative of down-to-earth Han realism, and one of its principal protaganists was Wang Ch'ung, who repudiated the idea that

Right : The reverse side of a bronze mirror of the TLV type. The design comprises cosmological themes symbolising the Earth and the twelve terrestrial branches, surrounded by the animals of the four quarters. Eastern Han Dynasty

171

such catastrophes were Heaven's way of warning the Emperor. They were, he insisted with forceful logic, merely part of nature's pattern caused by imbalances in the climate and structure of the earth.

Wang Ch'ung's basically scientific, rational stance may be contrasted with that of the poet Ch'ü Yüan, whose attitude reflects the approach of others working in academic and semi-academic pursuits. For example, the field of mathematics witnessed much activity, especially in the development of various measuring devices, for both time and distance. The sun-dial was first used in the second century BC. In this early example of a timepiece, the entire day and night was divided into a hundred sections which in turn related to twelve time periods (of two hours each). These were then denoted by descriptive terms such as 'cock-crow' and 'sunset'. Moments in time could therefore be more precisely pinpointed by reference to the hundred sections, for example 'sunset and six sections'.

Han mathematicians also formulated measurements of distance, in two principal units; the foot, which approximated to ten inches in our terms; and the *chang* equivalent to ten feet (thus approximately one hundred inches). From this, mathematicians applied themselves to the task of measuring areas, volumes and weights. Among the more ambitious scientific achievements of a Han scientist was a primitive seismograph in which the shock would swing a

Above : Storage or wine jar of stoneware with incised designs under a greygreen glaze. Eastern Han Dynasty
Above right : Pottery tomb figure of a mythical bird carrying on its wings two tripod vessels, ting, *accompanied by*

two officials. Eastern Han Dynasty
Right : Pottery tomb model of a lady. Han Dynasty
Over : Bronze tripod vessel with a duck's-head handle. Western Han Dynasty

pendulum set inside a bronze jar-like device. Once set in motion the pendulum would dislodge another arm attached to one of eight articulated dragons; this arm thus opened the jaws of the dragon from which a ball dropped into the jaws of a frog set on the base of the device. Thus the sound alerted the scientist and also indicated the direction.

Great strides were also made in the field of medicine and the diagnosis of diseases. Naturally the remedies were generally herbal, but alchemists were also concocting drugs. Another of Wang Mang's hopeful petitioners offered his services thus: '. . . that without carrying a measure of grain and by taking drugs, the three divisions of any army would not become hungry'.

One of the more remarkable features of Han medicine is indicated by some stone engravings recently found in Shantung province. A series of pictures show a strange mythological creature with human head and arms and the body and legs of a bird wielding what looks to be a hammer directed at the 'patient's' arm. These are without doubt early representations of one of the most fascinating aspects of Far Eastern medical science, acupuncture. It seems fitting that the earliest pictorial representations of this mysterious technique, the discovery of which is traditionally attributed to the legendary Emperor, Huang-ti, should date from the adventurous Han period.

9 THE LEGACY OF HAN

THE ACHIEVEMENT OF THE HAN DYNASTY IN ESTABLISHING THE first, strong centralised Chinese Empire can best be appreciated in the context of the subsequent history of China, and by contrast with the scattered feudal kingdoms of the preceding Bronze Age. The founding emperor, Kao Tsu, and his successors achieved no less than the formulation and establishment of a system of government and a social structure that were to remain basically the same for over two thousand years, until the collapse of the Imperial system in 1911.

Prince Liu Sheng, King of Chung-shan, lived during one of the most significant eras in the history of China. Although we may not be able to estimate his particular contribution, which, on the evidence of the Chinese historians, was hardly substantial, he none the less was high in the hierarchy which established and managed that system.

The rulers of the Han also established and defined China's spheres of influence. In the Shang and Chou periods China was the major cultural influence among the non-Chinese tribes of the steppe lands of Mongolia and the desert wastes and plains of Central Asia. During the Han, although China's political influence often extended across vast areas to the north and west of her original borders, she was confronted in those regions with the cultures of Indian, Near Eastern and Mediterranean civilisations. And we have seen how, instead of substantially influencing the cultures of these areas she occupied, China borrowed and accepted ideas and concepts. It was only in the east and south-east, in what are now Korea, Vietnam and Japan, that Chinese culture acquired an extensive sphere of influence, and one which is still evident today.

The outstanding distinguishing feature of all these Chinese-influenced areas was the use of the Chinese script, although we also see in these countries constant reference to the art of the Middle Kingdom. The written language was a vital acquisition for these 'satellite' countries, for it provided the educated classes with access to Chinese literature, to the works of the great pre-Han philosophers, and to Confucian conceptions of government and society, filial piety and respect, traditional ritual and ceremony, ancestor worship and, in the Later Han and after, to Buddhist texts.

In the formulation and execution of government we have seen how the Han employed the fundamental Confucian ethic of 'benevolent' rule within the framework of a strictly regulated hierarchy. At the top, the emperor was

Previous page : A set of five wooden figures from Mawangtui, playing musical instruments

alienated, and surrounded by an aura of divine mystery which maintained his position as the 'Son of Heaven'. Although his counsel should be sought and his influence felt, it was commonly held that he should not trouble himself with specific and trifling issues, but leave such cares and the daily routine of government to the care of his ministers. Thus the emperor could remain inflexibly faithful to certain basic principles, as he must if he were to embody his divine function of being the medium between Heaven and Earth. The adjusting and manipulating of laws, rules and principles should be left to his ministers and officials.

The position of the Emperor in Imperial China is graphically described in the *Huai-nan Tzu*, an Early Han philosophical work:

The craft of the ruler consists in disposing of affairs without action and issuing orders without speaking. The ruler remains still and pure without moving, impartial without wavering. Compliantly he delegates affairs to his subordinates and without troubling himself exacts success from them. Thus though he has plans in his mind, he allows his counsellors to proclaim them; though his mouth can speak, he allows his administrators to talk for him; though his feet can walk, he lets his ministers lead; and though he has ears to hear, he permits the officials to remonstrate with him. Thus among his policies are none that fail and among his plans are none that go astray . . .

It had been proved in the Ch'in that Legalist absolutism, like the earlier old-fashioned Confucianism which clung to ancient institutions, was unacceptable in an age of material wealth and contact with new peoples and civilisations. The greatest achievement of the Han was in the selection, adaptation and employment of ideas and concepts from Confucianism, Legalism and the other schools of thought and fusing them into a workable and, as it turned out, durable system.

So durable that the Han system of government was that employed by the great T'ang Dynasty (618–906 AD), the thoroughly Chinese Sung (960–1279 AD) and Ming (1368–1644) Dynasties, and even the last Imperial era, the Ch'ing Dynasty (1644–1911). The strength and tenacity of the system, within the framework of an Imperial constitution, is illustrated by the fact that the Ch'ing was not a Chinese but a Manchu Dynasty. These people had previously occupied territories to the north of China proper, but had been constantly within the Chinese sphere of influence and their adoption of Chinese ideals, both cultural and social, was a natural step for them to take when they overran the Middle Kingdom. 177

Fundamental to the Confucian doctrine, and thus the structure of society, was the concept of filial piety. Although an important feature of Bronze Age China, the concept became firmly established as part of the social order during the Han, and has remained so ever since. Respect for one's elders, not necessarily one's parents, and the care of the aged is a concept of basic morality extolled in China today. Under the Imperial system, however, it had a more precise meaning and function, for as Confucius said, 'Filial piety is the basis of virtue and the source of all instruction.' The lesson was that only after one had learned to serve one's parents with respect and obedience could one fulfil the duties to the Emperor and society in general.

The political consequences of the application of this doctrine were not always entirely satisfactory – as we saw, there were often conflicts of loyalties when the emperor was advised to act one way by his counsellors and entreated to act another by his mother, the Empress Dowager. Emperors often publicly honoured their mothers, by rewarding feoffs and kingdoms to their relatives, or even giving them high government posts. But the concept of filial piety was thoroughly instilled into the Chinese way of life, and persisted to the very end of the Imperial Age, as the antics and opportunism of the Empress Dowager Tzu Hsi in the late nineteenth and early twentieth centuries illustrate.

In the field of practical government the Han instituted many new policies, based on the doctrine of a strong centralised government and delegated local authority. This system enabled the Imperial government to maintain effective control but not to be burdened with tiresome day-to-day work. The establishment of that characteristically Confucian class of public servants, the officials or *Chün-tzu*, in the Han period subsequently produced one of the most consistently powerful and élitist groups of civil servants the world has ever known, the mandarins. In times of weak leadership from the Imperial throne these men attained immense power and wealth; never more so than in the failing years of the Ch'ing Dynasty in the nineteenth century.

The Confucian ethic also produced a morality of its own which, once formulated in the Han Dynasty, became accepted tenets of Chinese thought and society. First, there was the recognition that all men were not born equal. The lowly peasant could never be equated with the Son of Heaven, or the nobility. The three-tier structure of Han society, comprising emperor, officials and people, was successfully maintained throughout China's Imperial history.

Second, the Confucian bias towards a classical education established both the criteria and the need for a specialised and highly distinctive educational system, in which the study of the ancients featured prominently. The study and observance of Confucian and pre-Confucian Classics were the principal courses in the government-sponsored university for potential civil servants set up in the second century BC. This pattern was followed, too, by subsequent dynasties and established and maintained the respectful attitude towards the 'ancients' and, of course, the Classics. Even in painting the tradition was to study and to copy, as precisely as possible, the great masters of the past.

Third, with such a well-defined framework, both in social and governmental structures, so the component units themselves developed their own self-sustaining characteristics. Provincial and local units of political power acquired a degree of autonomy in their handling of day-to-day affairs. Once again the role of the official, and later the mandarin, classes in this respect was paramount.

During the height of Han power in the late first century AD, the Chinese Empire was at its largest, except for a short period of Mongol rule, during the Yüan Dynasty (1279–1368), and the successful devolution of power from central to local authority was vital to the maintenance of the Dynasty. Driven by sheer necessity the Han officials achieved a solution which characterised China for the next two thousand years, and inevitably left its mark on the nature of its society. For in a society with such a well-defined class structure, within a similarly well-defined social and governmental hierarchy, the barriers between classes tended to be forever strengthened.

Another consequence of the immense size of both the Empire and the population was the need to organise labour and production. The fulfilment of the demands of the central government, through its agencies the local authorities, in the form of taxes and produce had to be thoroughly organised

and protected. Thus the government encouraged the formation of collectives and co-operatives in the Han Dynasty, for it was easier to collect from one local source than from each individual farmer. Indeed the farmers and producers often formed collectives on their own initiative, as an insurance against the ravages of nature, or war. Thus there developed a sense of collective responsibility, and to some extent the subjugation of the 'cult of the individual' – certainly qualities very much in evidence in China today. For example we only seldom learn of individual artists or craftsmen; their names are not recorded nor their works signed. Only painters were known by their names, as the art was equated with calligraphy and the Classics, but the less esoteric arts and crafts – pottery, lacquer, sculpture and bronze-casting – were all created in anonymity.

These qualities and characteristics which evolved in the Han period remained constant features of Chinese society. The first cracks in this distinguished and respectable façade occurred in the late eighteenth century and in the nineteenth century when increasing contact with foreign barbarians, particularly the expansionist, mercantile powers of Europe, placed an immense strain on an already dying tradition, a weakening and thus corruptible Imperial house, and a country sliding into abject poverty. Then the Chinese were forced to face the harsh realities of a world of commerce, trade and industry beyond the Middle Kingdom.

Wealthy European countries saw China as a haven of exploitation in which they would reap huge profits from the sale of their fine silks and raw materials. When the impatience of the European merchants, entrepreneurs and politicians came face to face with the reticence and imperious suspicion of the Chinese hierarchy, clashes were inevitable. The Opium War of 1840 and the Boxer Uprising of 1900, an anti-foreign rebellion inspired by the Empress Dowager Tzu Hsi, were among the worst of these.

During this period China was increasingly suffering from a dying, corrupt and more and more withdrawn Imperial house. The country's resources were being plundered by the Western industrial countries, and what profits there were went immediately to help replenish the Imperial coffers. The wars with the Europeans resulted in immense losses to China, and in addition they were forced to give indemnities and territorial rights to the invaders. China became poverty-stricken and her people a starving mass without hope. The first great revolution in Chinese history occurred with the establishing of the

Previous page : Rubbing from a stone relief depicting a snake and a tortoise, the symbol of the north. From a tomb at Lu-shan in Sinkiang (Chinghai). Han Dynasty

Right : Model of the earliest known Chinese seismograph. When activated by an earth tremor, the jaws of the dragons open, releasing bronze balls which drop into the mouths of the toads below

Ch'in and Han Dynasties in the third century BC. The second occurred in 1911 with the overthrow of the Imperial system. China subsequently entered a period of internal conflict and readjustment, the tensions and strife greatly aggravated by persistent intrusions from the West, Russia and Japan, all of them eager to carve new territories and wealth out of a disintegrating China.

That China has emerged from these troubles and is now in the process of re-establishing herself as an independent and self-sufficient power is as it should be. But even today, under the socialist leadership of the People's Republic, certain qualities which were characteristic of Han society remain fundamental to China: a centralised government with local autonomous units operating within the over-all structure, the sense of collective responsibility, the desire for self-sufficiency, and above all a stoic refusal to be influenced substantially by external events and factors. The law of self-determination which inspired the building of the great Han Empire, persists to this day as a basic tenet of the people of China.

182 *Map of modern China, showing provincial boundaries, autonomous regions and principal cities.*

Over : Map of ancient China, circa *third century BC to the third century AD, showing the expansion of the Empire during the Chi'in and Han Dynasties*

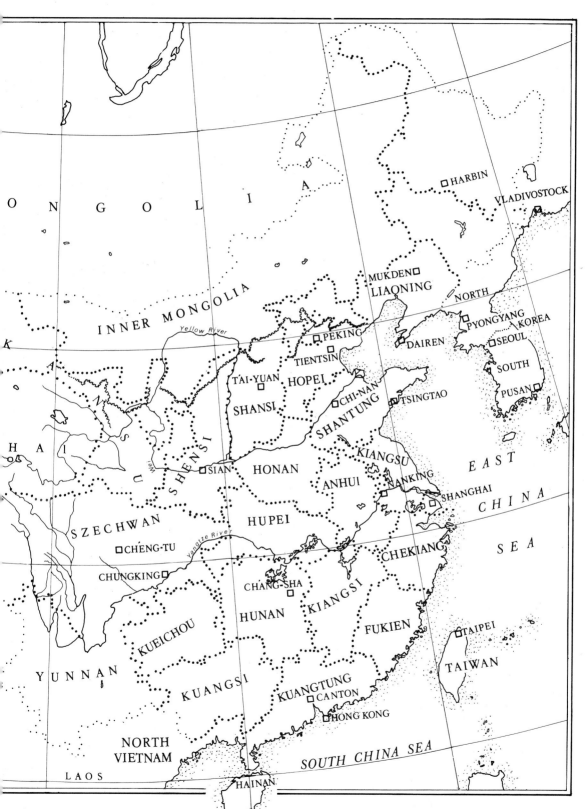

M O N G O L I A

INNER MONGOLIA

Yellow River

□ HARBIN

VLADIVOSTOCK

MUKDEN □
LIAONING

NORTH

PEKING □

TIENTSIN □

□ PYONGYANG
KOREA

DAIREN □

□ SEOUL

SOUTH

□ PUSAN

TAI-YUAN □
HOPEI

SHANSI

CHI-NAN □
SHANTUNG

□ TSINGTAO

SIAN □
HONAN

KIANGSU

SHENSI

ANHUI

NANKING □

□ SHANGHAI

EAST

CHINA

SZECHWAN

HUPEI

Yangtze River

CHENG-TU □

CHEKIANG

SEA

CHUNGKING □

CHANG-SHA □

HUNAN
KIANGSI

FUKIEN

□ TAIPEI

KUEICHOU

TAIWAN

YUNNAN

KUANGSI

KUANGTUNG
□ CANTON

□ HONG KONG

NORTH
VIETNAM

SOUTH CHINA SEA

LAOS

HAINAN

183

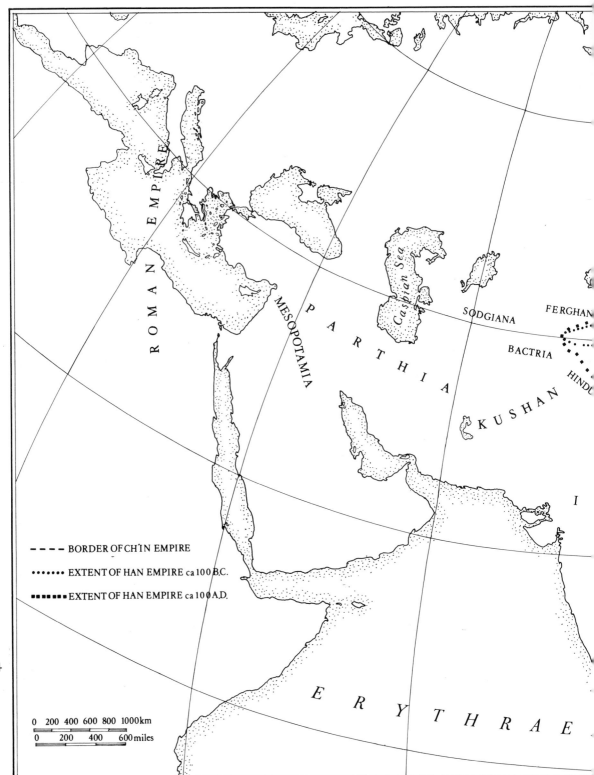

ROMAN EMPIRE

MESOPOTAMIA

P A R T H I A

Caspian Sea

SODGIANA

FERGHAN

BACTRIA

HINDU

K U S H A N

I

E R Y T H R A E

- - - - BORDER OF CH'IN EMPIRE

•••••• EXTENT OF HAN EMPIRE ca 100 B.C.

▪▪▪▪▪▪ EXTENT OF HAN EMPIRE ca 100 A.D.

184

0   200 400 600 800 1000 km

0   200   400   600 miles

GOBI DESERT

MANCHURIA

YÜ-MEN

PEKING

CHOU-KOU-TIEN
MAN-CHENG
AN-YANG

CHI-NAN

△ T'AI SHAN

PYONGYANG
SEOUL

LAN-CHOU

CHENG-CHOU
LO-YANG

SHANGHAI

WEI

CHANG-AN

YANGTZE

CHENG-TU

CHANG-SHA

TAIWAN

HONG KONG

A Y A S

D   I   A

S E A

185

Chronological Lists

CHRONOLOGICAL LIST OF THE DYNASTIES

Hsia Dynasty (legendary)	*circa* 2000–1500 BC
Shang Dynasty	*circa* 1500–1027
Western Chou Dynasty	1027– 770
Eastern Chou Dynasty	771– 221
Spring and Autumn (Ch'un Ch'iu) period	722– 481
Warring States period	481– 221
Ch'in Dynasty	221– 206
Western Han Dynasty	206 BC– AD 8
Hsin Dynasty (Wang Mang)	AD 9– 25
Eastern Han Dynasty	25– 220
Six Dynasties	221– 589
Sui Dynasty	581– 618
T'ang Dynasty	618– 906
Five Dynasties	907– 960
Sung Dynasty	960–1279
Yüan Dynasty	1279–1368
Ming Dynasty	1368–1644
Ch'ing Dynasty	1644–1911
Republic	1911–1949
People's Republic	1949–

186

THE HAN EMPERORS

Kao Tsu	206–195 BC
Hui	195–188
(Empress of Kao Tsu 188–180)	
Wen	180–157
Ching	157–141
Wu	141– 87
Chao	87– 74
Hsüan	74– 48
Yüan	48– 33
Ch'eng	33– 7
Ai	7– 1
P'ing	1 BC–AD 6
Wang Mang	AD 9– 23
Kuang	25– 58
Ming	58– 76
Chang	76– 89
Ho	89–106
Shang	106–107
An	107–126
Shun	126–145
Ch'ung	145–146
Chih	146–147
Huan	147–168
Ling	168–189
Shao	189
Hsien	189–220

Left : Rubbing of a Han stone relief picture found in Shantung province, depicting early acupuncture technique

Select Bibliography

AKIYAMA, T. and others, *Arts of China Vol. I; Neolithic Cultures to the T'ang Dynasty. Recent Discoveries*, Tokyo 1968

BACHHOFER, L., *A Short History of Chinese Art*, New York 1946

CHÊNG TÊ-K'UN, *Archaeology in China. Vol. I Prehistoric China*, (Supplement to Vol. I: *New Light in Prehistoric China.* 1959): *Vol. II Shang China : Vol. III Chou China*, Cambridge 1959–63

CHINA: CULTURAL PROPERTIES COMMISSION, *Wen-hua ta-hua-ming ch'i-chien ch'u-t'u wen-wu* (Cultural relics unearthed during the Great Cultural Revolution), Peking 1972

CHINA: FOREIGN LANGUAGES PRESS, *Cultural Relics Unearthed in New China*, Peking 1972

CREEL, H. G., *The Birth of China.* 4th ed., New York 1961

DUBS, H. H., *The History of the Former Han Dynasty* (by Pan Ku) 3 vols, Baltimore and London 1938–55

EBERHARD, W., *A History of China*, London 1950

FITZGERALD, C. P., *China : A Short Cultural History*, London 1961

FUNG YU-LAN, *A Short History of Chinese Philosophy* (ed. by D. Bodde), New York 1960

HERRMAN, A., *An Historical Atlas of China*, Edinburgh 1966

HUNAN PROVINCIAL MUSEUM, *Ch'ang-sha ma-wang tui i-hao han-mu fa-chüeh chien-pao* (Report on the excavation of the Han tomb at Mawangtui, Ch'ang-sha), Peking 1972

LATOURETTE, K. S., *The Chinese : Their Culture and History*, New York 1964

LATTIMORE, O., *Inner Asian Frontiers of China*, New York 1964

LI CHI, *The Beginnings of Chinese Civilisation*, Seattle 1967

LOEWE, M., *Everyday Life in Early Imperial China*, London 1968

NEEDHAM, J., *Science and Civilisation in China,* Vols I–IV, Cambridge 1954–72

RUDOLPH, R. C., *Han Tomb Art of West China*, Berkeley and Los Angeles 1951

REISCHAUER, E. O., and FAIRBANK, J. K., *East Asia : The Great Tradition*, Boston 1960

SICKMAN, L., and SOPER, A. C., *The Art and Architecture of China*, London (Pelican) 1956, 3rd ed. 1968

WALEY, A., *Three Ways of Thought in Ancient China*, London 1946

WATSON, B., *Records of the Grand Historian of China.* (Translated from the *Shih-chi* by Ssu-ma Ch'ien) New York and London 1961

WATSON, W., *Handbook to the Collections of Early Chinese Antiquities in the British Museum*, London 1961

WATSON, W., *Early Civilisation in China*, London 1966

WATSON, W., *Cultural Frontiers in Ancient East Asia*, Edinburgh 1971

WILLETTS, W., *Chinese Art* 2 vols., Harmondsworth 1958

WRIGHT, A. F. (ed), *Studies in Chinese Thought*, Chicago 1953

WRIGHT, A. F. (ed), *The Confucian Persuasion*, Stanford 1960

INDEX

*Over : A detail from the painted silk
banner (see page 165) showing a
bird as the symbol of the sun*

Acknowledgements

The authors and publishers wish to express their thanks to the following, all of whom helped to make this book and its range of illustrations possible: Ashmolean Museum, Oxford, Trustees of the British Museum, Hsinhua News Agency, Luxingshe (Chinese Travel Service), Musée Cernuschi, Paris, Nanking Museum, Peking Museum, Petit Palais, Paris, Shanghai Museum, and the Victoria and Albert Museum. Our thanks also to the people of the People's Republic of China, who extended every possible help and kindness to the authors.

192